Paris Parks:
Poisons, Devils, and Duels

Paris Parks:
Poisons, Devils, and Duels

Historical Journeys in the
City of Light

James Bowers

ISBN: 978-0-578-85764-0

Senna Books

Printed in the United States of America

For Deborah

To Madame La Comtesse de Tesse
Nismes, March 20, 1787

"While in Paris, I was violently smitten with the Hôtel de Salm, and used to go to the Tuileries almost daily to look at it."

Madam, your most obedient and most humble servant,
Thomas Jefferson.

Table of Contents

Preface

Our plan for the day was to visit the Musée Cernuschi, one of the older museums in Paris specializing in Asian art. After an afternoon of viewing priceless treasures, my wife and I decided to meander our way back to our apartment through the elegant Parc Monceau. We had spent two months in Paris, and had increasingly enjoyed our strolls through the many parks and gardens dotting the city.

Along a small path running through the park was an inconspicuous sign stating, *Allée Jacques Garnerin Premier Parachutiste 1769–1823*. I thought to myself, "what was that all about?" That evening I read about Monsieur Garnerin in the Wikipedia Encyclopedia. Although most students of French history are already well read on the Montgolfier brothers, who with their hot air balloon, were the first humans to leave the Earth, I was unaware that the first human to free fall and parachute back to Earth also did so in Paris, in this case the Parc Monceau. Having made a few parachute jumps myself, I appreciated his outsized courage taken in 1797.

Continued visits to the parks revealed further historical events. I learned that Paris is sometimes called, "The City of 400 Gardens", and in 1994 Paris listed 397 gardens and parks, 102 small green spaces called "jarinets", and 411 even smaller "decorations."

More and more my wanderings focused on these green spaces. I read everything I could find on the subject, scouring Paris bookstores and finding sources from the general catalogue of the Bibliothèque nationale. I discovered that one of the city's official publications, *Les parcs et jardins de Paris*, makes a clear point of coupling Paris history to its parks and gardens. Anne Soprani's delightful, *Paris Jardins: Promenade historique dans les parcs and jardins de chaque arrondissement*, supplied even more information on the role parks and gardens played in the building and shaping of Paris.

After several years of researching the topic, I realized there were no specific studies of the topic beyond Soprani's book, which focuses mainly on the larger more visited parks and was not available in English. The solution? To write one myself. I loved writing this book. I hope it is enjoyable to read.

Acknowledgements

I am grateful to many people and institutions for making this search into the history of Paris a reality. No one deserves more accolades than the people of Paris. Their constant kindness and assistance with directions, local knowledge of a neighborhood, and inspirational support made it all quite an adventure.

The Internet has revolutionized how information is disseminated in the world and no organization has accomplished more than the Wikimedia Foundation's Wikipedia Encyclopedia. Both the English and French encyclopedias guided my early research of the historical literature. The University of South Carolina-Aiken Library, Augusta State University Library, and the City Library of Columbia, South Carolina were all extremely helpful in providing historical texts and interlibrary loans. In Paris I thank the American Library of Paris, the Bibliothèque Historique de la Ville de Paris (BHVP), and the Bibliothèque nationale de France (BnF).

Drs. Steve Bank and Laurie Talalay helped shape the very nature of these essays. Dr. Kathy Talalay's advice on the structure and formatting of the book was invaluable. Gregory Messina provided valuable assistance in editing the text.

I thank my wife Deborah for the illustrations. Her continuous support gave me the freedom to initiate, sustain, and complete the writing.

Introduction — How to Use This Book

On October 11, 1795 the National Convention abolished the municipal government of Paris and divided the city into twelve districts called *arrondissements municipaux*. The government of France was in no mood for unruly Paris to possess any consolidated power given the tumultuous events during the Revolution. After Paris grew in size the original twelve arrondissements increased to twenty. They are spatially arranged in a clockwise snail-like spiral beginning along the Seine at the heart of the city.

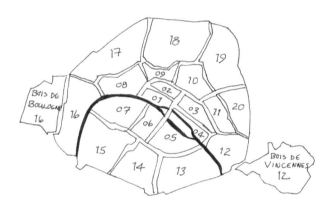

Arrondissements of Paris

This book contains twenty chapters, each discussing a park or garden. They are presented in the order in which they are located in the arrondissements. At the end of each chapter, a small section indicates which metro takes you to the park or garden, which stop to use, or the street coordinates. It also includes information for those readers visiting the park such as other nearby places of interest or additional activities in the park. A bibliography of the source material is presented. A chronology outlines the sequence of historical events.

Several of the chapters contain quotes written over two hundred years ago. I have not altered any of the English quotes often written in eighteenth-century English where spelling and grammar differs from current usage. Quotes in English that were translated from the original French were also not altered, as I wanted the reader to experience the exact English of the original reference. Any errors in the text are my own.

The author and Deborah Sandberg-Bowers took all of the photographs. Deborah Sandberg-Bowers also created all of the drawings.

Paris Parks — Poisons, Devils, and Duels was conceived not only as an historical narrative, but as a tribute to the green spaces of Paris. During my first visit to the Palais-Royal garden in 1991, I remember resting on a park bench and thinking, "Goodness, I'm sitting where Napoleon, Franklin, Colette, Camus, and Hemmingway sat!"

Chapter 1. Jardins du Palais-Royal

"What is this world? A complex whole, subject to endless revolutions."
(1)
Denis Diderot (1713–1784)

Today the tranquil gardens of the Palais-Royal are the antithesis of what they were in the late eighteenth century during an explosive moment in world history, the French Revolution.

A singularity in cosmology is defined as that moment when the density of the universe was infinite and the traditional laws of physics no longer applied. For a single moment in the history of France there came to be what I term an historical singularity where all of the societal forces of the French nation collapsed into a single location with near infinite force. After centuries of despotic rule under the Bourbon monarchy, this autocratic police state exploded in its own Big Bang. The point of origin was the Palais-Royal and its gardens. Ironically, the principal architect of the Bourbon autocracy created the palace and gardens.

Armand-Jean du Plessis was born on September 9, 1585, the fourth of five children to François du Plessis, a Grand Provost of France under Henry IV. Following in his father's footsteps, Armand-Jean began a career in the military. Fate intervened, when his older brother Alphonse turned down an offer to become the bishop of Luçon. His family forced Armand-Jean to become a clergyman. Ambitious, he threw himself into his new role in life and by April 1607, Pope Paul V consecrated Armand-Jean as Bishop of Luçon. Armand-Jean's rise was astonishing; by 1616 Marie de Médici, Queen Regent of France, named him Secretary of State. In 1622 Louis XIII had Pope Gregory XV promote Armand-Jean to Cardinal de Richelieu. On August 12, 1624 Louis appointed him First Minister of State. Given his new position the Cardinal desired a suitable new home.

Marie de Médici built her Tuileries Palace close to the Louvre to watch over her two sons. Cardinal Richelieu set his new palace also near the Louvre to watch over the French state. In 1624 Richelieu purchased the old Hôtel d'Argennes-Rambouillet. In 1639 after nine years of construction the Palais-Cardinal, as it was first named, was completed with a formal garden he called his *parc*. Surprisingly, Richelieu opened it to the public. As noted in Louis Petit de Bachaumont's (1690–1771) *Mémoires secrets*, the gardens of the Palais-Royal were to become one of the most famous meeting places in the history of France.

July 1636: Spanish armies threaten Paris during the Thirty Years War

The Thirty Years War was in its eighteenth year. Germany was being annihilated with Württemberg losing three-fourths of her population and Brandenburg losing an estimated one-half of its citizens. Richelieu's policy of supporting Protestant Sweden and German states kept the war far from Paris. Nonetheless, by 1635 several Protestant German states sued for peace with the Catholic Holy Roman Empire. Sweden could not continue alone even with considerable French subsidies.

In May 1635 France entered the war against Catholic Spain and declared war on the Holy Roman Empire the following year. In July 1636 Catholic German general Johann von Werth and Spanish General Cardinal-Infante Ferdinand scored several victories over French armies and threatened the very gates of Paris. Parisians panicked and readied themselves to defend the city. Richelieu's Palais-Cardinal and its gardens became an object of controversy.

In 1633 Louis XIII had started to reinforce the old city walls built by Charles V, but Richelieu had torn down part of the wall alongside the Palais-Cardinal to make room for his palace and gardens. The Cardinal foolishly filled in the defensive moat. Local Parisians were furious. Fortunately, Paris was saved when Protestant German general Bernhard von Sachsen-Weimar won the Battle of Compiègne pushing the Spanish forces back north to the French border. The wall stayed down.

May 14, 1642: Louis XIII dies and Anne of Austria moves into the Palais-Royal

Anne of Austria became Queen Regent of France on the death of Louis XIII, and took great pleasure in taking possession of the private apartments of her old enemy, Cardinal Richelieu.

During the Regency her two sons, the future Louis XIV and Philippe I, the Duke of Orléans lived in the Palais-Royal. Both small boys grew up playing in the garden under the watchful eye of their tutor Monsieur de Villeroy. Left on his own, little Louis once fell in the pond and nearly drowned. When the future king was twelve years old, Anne built a small fort in the gardens with bastions, moats, and redoubts for the boys to play soldiers.

1715: Decadence at the Palais-Royal: The Regency of Philippe d'Orleans

After seventy-two years of rule Louis XIV died in 1715 with the five-year-old Louis XV becoming king. The Duke of Orléans became Regent, whereupon the seat of power transferred from Versailles to the Duke's home in the Palais-Royal.

The Duke was dedicated to an epicurean lifestyle and the Palais-Royal now became famous for rowdy evening parties. Saint-Simon in his *Memoirs of Louis XIV and Court and of the Regency* recorded the wild parties the Duke held with friends after business hours. Besides aristocratic friends the Duke often entertained lower ranked men and women noted for their love of shared debaucheries.

Marc de Voyer, the Marquis d'Argenson (1722–1787) noted art and book collector, lived near the Palais-Royal said this of the palace and its gardens. "I have never seen a little village so vexatious that is the Palais-Royal. This is today, and according to the politeness of the century, a den of gossip, slander, repetition, bad paintings, and detestable writings."

James Bowers

1762: Denis Diderot, encyclopedist and flâneur in the Palais-Royal garden

Diderot, writing in *Rameau's Nephew* (1762), offers personal daydreams regarding his wanderings in the Palais-Royal gardens.

"No matter what the weather, rain or shine, it's my habit every evening at about five o'clock to take a walk around the Palais-Royal. I'm the one you see dreaming on the bench in Argenson's Alley, always alone. I talk to myself about politics, love, taste, or philosophy. I let my spirit roam at will, allowing it to follow the first idea, wise or foolish, which presents itself, just as we see our dissolute young men on Foy's Walk following in the footsteps of a prostitute with a smiling face, an inviting air, and a turned-up nose, then leaving her for another, going after all of them and sticking to none. For me, my thoughts are my prostitutes."

"If the weather is too cold or too rainy, I take refuge in the Regency Café. I like to watch the games of chess. The best chess players in the world are in Paris, and the best players in Paris are in the Regency Café. Here, in Rey's establishment, they battle it out—Legal the Profound, Philidor the Subtle, Mayot the Solid. One sees the most surprising moves and hears the stupidest remarks. For one can be an intelligent man and a great chess player, like Legal, but one can also be a great chess player and a fool, like Foubert and Mayot."

1781: The first strip-mall? Louis Philippe II creates the commercial and social center of Paris in the Palais-Royal.

The Duke was broke. Louis Philippe II, the Duke d'Orléans, known during and after the Revolution as Philippe-Égalité, began in 1781, and completed in 1784, a larger more complex Palais-Royal with spaces for rent. Louis XVI was to have commented on the construction. "I suppose now that you are going to keep shop, cousin, we shall see you only on Sundays?"

Jardins du Palais-Royal

When completed, this eighteenth-century colonnade contained at least 145 shops. Having two stories, the upper level had the gambling halls and brothels, while the downstairs had the cafes, meeting halls, and shops of all types. What made this new reconstructed palace unique was the patronage by all levels of society, from the nobility to the lowest classes in Paris.

Several cafes experienced some of the most sophisticated political discourses in western civilization, all the while a favorite hangout of neighborhood prostitutes. This mélange of French society, unique to time and place, was about to host history. Anne-Henri Cabot, Vicomte de Dampmartin, predicted this historical singularity stating, "the Palais-Royal is so instrumental in the kingdom that nineteenth-century historians will have to study it very carefully, and maybe they will be able to disentangle all the forces hidden there."

1782–1788 : Louis-Sébastien Mercier's description of Palais-Royal in the Le Tableau de Paris

"They call it the capitol of Paris. Everything is to be found there; a young man with twenty years of life behind him and fifty thousand francs in his pocket need never leave it, nor even wish to, like Rinaldo in the palace of Armida; but whereas that legendary hero only lost time and fame, our present-day swan would probably lose all his money as well; besides forming such a habit of the place, that he could never be really happy elsewhere."

On the Thursday evening of November 22, 1787, eighteen-year-old Napoleon Bonaparte attended the Comédie Italienne and enjoyed a suggestive light operetta entitled, Berthe et Pépin. The night was still young. Strolling through the gardens of the Palais-Royal Bonaparte met up with a young woman he escorted back to the Hôtel de Cherbourg, where the future Emperor of France lost his virginity.

1781–1794: A tour of shops in the Palais-Royal arcades before, during, and after the Revolution

Let us walk around the gardens, enter the columned entrances, and visit the more famous establishments in Palais-Royal history.

Doctor Philippe Curtius, a physician from Switzerland, came to Paris in 1765. He brought anatomical wax creations of the human body for medical study. These life-like wax creations were immediately successful whereupon he opened the Curtius wax museum at Number 7 in the Palais-Royal. On the night Louis XVI dismissed France's financial advisor Necker, M. Curtius created wax busts of Monsieur Necker and the Duke de Orléans for the multitude to parade through the streets in protest to the king. In 1785 a permanent museum was built at Number 17 and stayed in business until 1847.

Madame Tussaud, who had accompanied Curtius from Switzerland, took over the business, and in 1835 founded her famous wax museum in London.

Established in 1787 the Café Glacier Corazza in the Galerie de Montpensier occupied Numbers 7 through 12 at various periods. It was a favorite hangout of Napoleon Bonaparte and the Jacobins during the Revolution.

Number 9 was infamous for its suicides by the losers at adjacent gambling houses.

Occupying Numbers 57, 59, and 60, the Café de Foy had a well-designed interior for discriminating clientele. On July 12, 1789, Louis XVI fired Finance Minister Necker thus outraging those French calling for reforms. The journalist Camille Desmoulins had witnessed the event at Versailles and brought the news to Parisians at the Café de Foy. Desmoulins leaped up upon a table and shouted to all his incendiary speech that helped launch the French Revolution.

The grand restaurant Le Véry at Numbers 83-86 opened its doors in 1808 and became the first Parisian eatery to offer what was to become ubiquitous to the catering business, the "fixed-price" menu.

Le Café des Aveugles (Cafe of the Blind), located at Number 10 Galerie de Beaujolais, was a popular nightspot for decades. Its fame derived from the small orchestra whose members were all blind. The musicians lived in the nearby Hospice of the Three Hundred which Saint Louis founded in 1260. An engraving in the Bibliothèque nationale de France dated September 1771, celebrates a grand concert extraordinaire at the Café des Aveugles. Honoré de Balzac was a frequent visitor to the café during the evenings. His good friend the romantic poet Gerard de Nerval wrote of the visits, "It was not too late. Our laziness made time appear to go slowly. In passing to Perron in order to cross the Palais-Royal, a loud noise drew our attention to the rowdiness which constant it's being at the Café des Aveugles."

At Numbers 106-112 in the Galerie de Valois, was the gambling house Petit-Véfour where many fortunes were lost on a single night. Downstairs was the Café Borel. An amateur ventriloquist, the owner Borel wandered amongst the tables amusing the clientele.

James Bowers

Jardins du Palais-Royal

Arcade in the Palais-Royal

"I have executed one man to save a hundred thousand."(2) Charlotte Corday allegedly spoke these words at her trial for stabbing to death Jean-Paul Marat. A radical journalist, Marat had supported the continued violence of the Revolution and approved of the September Massacres. At six o'clock in the morning July 13, 1793, Corday was pacing back and forth at the front door of a cutlery boutique located at Number 177. Monsieur Badin, the owner, finally arrived and opened the store. Minutes later Badin sold a six-inch knife to Corday, whereupon later in the day Corday managed to get an appointment with Marat at his home. At midday on the pretext she had information of a planned uprising by the Girondists in Caen, Corday entered Marat's home. Due to a debilitating skin condition, Marat spent the day in a bathtub where he conducted business. Corday began giving Marat information on the supposed uprising, while Marat took notes. Corday immediately stabbed Marat in the heart. Jacques-Louis David immortalized the scene in his painting *The Death of Marat*. Corday was guillotined at the Place de Concorde on July 17, 1793.

Established in 1784 the Restaurant Véfour began life as the Café de Chartres. Jean Véfour bought the restaurant in 1820. Through more than two centuries this eatery has entertained such luminaries as Napoleon and Josephine, George Sand, Victor Hugo, Colette, and Jean Cocteau. Situated in the galerie de Beaujolais, the Véfour remains one of the finer restaurants in Paris.

Let us end this tour of shops with the Café Mécanique. Some Japanese sushi restaurants serve their dishes on a conveyor belt for easy selection. The Café Mécanique had a similar conveyor belt which wound amongst the tables delivering drinks. It was located in the Arcade Tissot at Number 101 and opened on May 13, 1793.

December, 1784: The Duke of Chartres installs a cannon in the Palais-Royal garden.

When I first came upon the little cannon perched on the garden lawn of the Palais-Royal in 1995, I asked myself what it was doing there. This is the little cannon's life story.

Until December 1784 the large sundial in the garden of the Palais-Royal was a popular place for Parisians to set their watches or to read the time. Jean-

Dominique Cassini, the noted astronomer at the Royal Observatory, proposed to build a noon cannon in the garden, but the city forbade Cassini citing safety reasons for firing a cannon in the middle of the city. However, the Duke of Chartres ignored the city government, and installed a little cannon integrated with the sundial, where the sun's rays ignited the powder through a magnifying lens focused on the breech of the cannon. It was positioned precisely on the French prime meridian, equivalent to Great Britain's Greenwich prime meridian. A watchmaker, Monsieur Rousseau, who had a shop at number 95 Galerie de Beaujolais, assembled the cannon. Parisians set their watches by the midday firing of the little cannon from May through October. Jacques Abbé Delille (1738-1813), famous poet and classicist translator of the period wrote,

"Dans ce jardin on ne rencontre (In this garden one encounters)

Ni champs, ni prés, ni bois, ni fleurs. (neither fields nor meadows nor woods nor flowers)

Et si l'on y dérègle ses mœurs, (And, if one upsets one's morality)

Au moins on y règle sa montre. (at least one may re-set one's watch)." (3)

For twenty years the little cannon set the official time for France according to a law passed on March 15, 1891. Stolen in 1998, a replica was positioned in 2002, where it resides today.

1787: Louis-Philippe builds a race track in the Palais-Royal Garden

In 1787 Louis-Philippe d'Orleans once again was strapped for cash and created yet another entertainment scheme to entice locals and tourists. Louis built a small hippodrome for horse races in the exact center of the garden. Seventy-two Doric columns surrounded the track to blend into the surrounding facades. Besides horse racing, the hippodrome hosted puppet shows along with occasional plays and operas. The Théâtre du Musée des Enfants even put-on short stories for children. A common problem of the age, the track burned to the ground in 1799.

Storefront for the original Le Café Corrazza

Entrance to Restaurant Véfour

James Bowers

Palais-Royal gardens with the noonday cannon

January–July 1789: Life in the Palais-Royal just before the Revolution

Let us now set the stage for the French Revolution, hosted in part, by the Palais-Royal gardens. The classless ambiance in the cafes, restaurants, and saloons in the Palais-Royal provided the atmosphere for political and social groups to coalesce and rebel against the totalitarian state of Louis XVI. Historian Johannes Willms, author of *Paris: Capitol of Europe from the Revolution to the Belle Epoque*, emphasized the turbulent gatherings at the Palais-Royal. Willms likened the palace and gardens to an eye of a hurricane that would sweep away the Bourbon Regime.

June 1789: Travel writer Arthur Young witnesses the stormy gatherings in the Palais-Royal

Arthur Young, one of the greatest writers on agriculture in the English language, traveled in France from the years 1787 to 1789 studying working conditions throughout the country. His *Travels in France*, published in 1792, is still held for its inciteful portrayal of agriculture, economics, and social conditions in France under the Ancient Regime. Here are some observations at the Palais-Royal cafes and its gardens during the month of June 1789, when Parisians were nearing revolt over political and economic events.

Tuesday, June 9, 1789 – "The pamphlet shops working out of the Palais-Royal published thirteen news stories that day attacking the clergy and nobility and calling for liberty of French citizens. During the week before ninety-one similar pamphlets were sold on the streets. Many articles focused on people starving for the want of bread." (4)

Wednesday, June 24, 1789 – "Ten thousand French fill the garden and surrounding areas of the Palais-Royal to hear the news regarding events from the National Assembly and Estates General."

Friday, June 26, 1789 – "Pamphleteers and political activists openly propose the idea of a free constitution and a republic. The garden was noisy late into the night with a large crowd well after 11:00 p.m." Young believed that the Duke d'Orléans was behind much of the proceedings."

Tuesday, June 30, 1789 – "The rumor for today was that Marie-Antoinette would be convicted for plotting to assassinate her husband Louis XVI and offer the regency to Count d'Artois his brother. Furthermore, the plot also involved blowing up the Palais-Royal!"

July 1789: The author Chamfort witnesses the coming of the Revolution

Sébastien-Roch Nicolas, writing under the pen name of Chamfort, lived at number 18, Arcades du Palais-Royal. Working as secretary to Louis XVI's sister, Elisabeth of France, Chamfort became famous for his insightful observations. This quote brings the ferocity of the Revolution right before our eyes.

"In six minutes you could suppose yourself in a smoking room, a dancehall, a fair grounds, a harem, and an armed camp. The disorder let to a general stupefaction, and the confusion of ideas made me think at once of Athens and Constantinople, Sybaris and Algiers. Suddenly a new sound was heard: the drum! The drum calling for silence. Two torches, waved high in the air, drew all eyes towards them. And what we saw! A severed bleeding head, held full in the ghastly torchlight, with a man walking in front and crying out in a dismal voice, 'Make way for the people's justice!' and everyone watching without a word! And not many yards away the evening patrol, in uniform, took notice of all what was going on and marched in silence among the astonished multitude." (5)

Chamfort, a dedicated Jacobian republican, embraced the French Revolution. A participant at the storming of the Bastille, Chamfort himself became a victim of the Terror. Arrested twice and fearing another arrest he attempted suicide in September, 1793, and finally died a painful death on April 13, 1794.

2:30 p.m., Sunday, July 12, 1789: Camille Desmoulins shouts a "call to arms" sparking the attack on the Bastille and the beginning of the French Revolution.

Camille Desmoulins, a lawyer turned journalist, followed events closely at the Estates General. When Louis XVI discharged Jacques Necker, the reform minded finance minister, many believed the king was about to send mercenary troops to Paris and arrest any political dissenters. Here are Desmoulins's actions written by eyewitness Thomas Carlyle in 1837.

"Rumour, therefore, shall arise; in the Palais-Royal, and in broad France. Paleness sits on every face; confused tremor and fremescence; waxing into thunder-peals, of Fury stirred on by Fear.

But see Camille Desmoulins, from the Café de Foy, rushing out, sibylline in face; his hair streaming, in each hand a pistol! He springs to a table: the Police satellites are eyeing him; alive they shall not take him, not they alive him alive. This time he speaks without stammering: —Friends, shall we die like hunted hares? Like sheep hounded into their pinfold; bleating for mercy, where is no mercy, but only a whetted knife? The hour is come; the supreme hour of Frenchman and Man; when Oppressors are to try conclusions with

16

Oppressed; and the word is, swift Death, or Deliverance forever. Let such hour be well-come! Us, meseems, one cry only befits: To Arms! Let universal Paris, universal France, as with the throat of the whirlwind, sound only: To arms! —'To arms!' yell responsive the innumerable voices: like one great voice, as of a Demon yelling from the air: for all faces wax fire-eyed, all hearts burn up into madness. In such, or fitter words, does Camille evoke the Elemental Powers, in this great moment. —Friends, continues Camille, some rallying sign! Cockades; green ones; —the colour of hope!—As with the flight of locusts, these green tree leaves; green ribands from the neighbouring shops; all green things are snatched, and made cockades of. Camille descends from his table, "stifled with embraces, wetted with tears;" has a bit of green riband handed him; sticks it in his hat. And now to Curtius' Image-shop there; to the Boulevards; to the four winds; and rest not till France be on fire!" (6)

Thursday July 16, 1789: Eyewitness to the Revolution Thomas Blaikie has a drink at the Café de Foy.

Living on the grounds of the Park Monceau, Scottish gardener Thomas Blaikie was the head gardener for the Duke of Chartres. Blaikie also held the same position for the Count d'Artois, brother of Louis XVI, at the Park Belleville. Two days after the storming of the Bastille, Blaikie was at the Café de Foy in the Palais-Royal watching the drama unfold. He recounted.

"All seemed quiet for the present and fetes given in Paris; went one evening to see one of those rejoissance (Old French for rejoice) in the Palais-Royal after went into the Caffe de Foix with three more acquaintance to take glass of liquor after the fete; the waiter seeing three men enter was so frightened that instead of filling our glasses he brought a bottle and told us to take what we pleased and so left us as in fright; we had some difficulty to reassure the poor fellow that he was mistaken and need not be afraid after that he became a little more reassured. About this time everyone was afraid of another and round the place groups of people some proposing one thing some another but few really knew what they wanted." (7)

1790: A Russian tourist at the Palais-Royal

At the end of the eighteenth century the Palais-Royal was one of Europe's most visited tourist locations, even during the lawlessness of the Revolution. One Russian tourist, Nikolai Karamzin, in the midst of this chaos wrote, "I spent five days like five hours in the noise, the crowd, the theatres, in the magic enclosure of the Palais-Royal. The Palais-Royal is called the heart, the soul, the brain, the précis of Paris." (8)

January 20, 1793: Revolutionary politician Le Peletier is assassinated at the Café Borel and becomes a character in a 21st century action video game.

The Convention had voted on January 17, 1793 to execute Louis XVI for conspiracy against the public liberty and the general safety of the state. The vote was not lopsided, 361 to execute, 288 against, and 72 to execute subject to a list of circumstances. Many voting for the execution were driven by the appearance of Louis conspiring with the governments of Prussia and the Holy Roman Empire, to attack France and reinstate Louis as king. According to the doctrine of the Brunswick Manifesto, first given to the French on August 1, 1792 by the Duke of Brunswick, any harm to Louis and his family provided a reason for war.

Three days later at the Café Borel, Philippe Nicolas Marie de Paris, a member of the disbanded Garde du Corps, drew a saber from beneath his coat and ran it through the chest of Michel Peletier, marquis de Saint-Fargeau and hero of the Revolution, as an act of revenge for Peletier's vote to execute. Jacques-Louis David captured the assassination in the painting, *Last Moments of Michel Peletier*. Given an elaborate state funeral, Peletier was interned in the Panthéon. Two hundred twenty-one years later Michel Peletier comes back as a character in an action-historical-drama video game set in revolutionary Paris, titled *Assassin's Creed Unity*.

May 31, 1799: The Comédie-Française moves into the Salle Richelieu at the Palais-Royal

Created in 1682 under the state patronage of Louis XIV, the Comédie-Française was moved in 1799 to its final home, where it resides today, the Salle Richelieu annex to the Palais-Royal. The only French state theater with a permanent staff of actors, the Comédie-Française theatrical company traces its history back to Pierre Molière's original Troupe de Molière, formed around 1648. The repertoire of the Comédie-Française was predominantly Molière's tragedies.

November 1810: Medical student, Poumiès de la Siboutie, describes the Palais-Royal during the reign of Napoleon Bonaparte.

Twenty-one-year-old Poumiès de la Siboutie had realized his dream of attending medical school in Paris. Born and raised in rural Périgord, Siboutie, as with many other newcomers to Paris, was quite amazed at the offerings of the Palais-Royal during Napoleonic France. He wrote.

"The Palais-Royal was the chief meeting-place of social Paris. Strangers flocked to see the wonderful bazaar; yet it had few of the attractions it offers now. At night it was lighted only by a few lanterns. The shops were dressed each according to its owner's individual taste, and presented a shocking incongruity; the wares overflowed into the Galleries, and hindered the movement of the crowd. In place of the Orléans and Nemours Galleries, there were only wooden sheds.

These were, however, a favorite meeting-ground in winter, and were full of people all day long. The Palais-Royal catered for all tastes: there could be found the best cafes and restaurants, two theaters, tumblers, ventriloquists. It was a world in miniature. There were three gaming-houses, each with its different set of patrons, from No. 113, where laborers might resort in their working clothes, to No. 124, where evening dress was indispensable. Admission was easy to obtain. In the outer room lounged half a dozen lusty fellows, called grooms of the chamber, who relieved would-be patrons of their weapons, walking-sticks, and hats. The apartments were large and handsome, furnished with comfortable seats and armchairs. Roulette, trente-et-quarante, biribi, and craps were played. Each game had its own hall." (9)

19

"At No. 124 dancing, called bal sentimental, took place every night, beginning at midnight and going on till four in the morning. The dancers were girls, young rakes, and, sad to relate, old libertines, who were always present in large numbers. Strangers also came, anxious to see Parisian life. Entrance and refreshments were free, but smart dressing was expected. Often when male partners were scarce the girls danced merrily with each other. Palais-Royal balls acted as traps for girls who had earned good money in the day, and young men who had dined well and carried well-lined pockets. The gaming room was next to the ballroom.

Comédie-Française, Palais-Royal

The girls were great gamblers: they dragged the men in between the dances, borrow their money, and when that was lost, set them to lay on their own account. Sometimes a youth who had merely strolled in out of curiosity lost every penny he had on him and walk out with the passion for gambling awakened in his soul. After all expenses were paid, this ball brought in a nightly profit of 3,000 to 4,000 francs for the management. I was present once, so what I describe I have seen with my own eyes. It came to an end in 1816."

Forty years later, Doctor Siboutie, now a distinguished physician in Paris, described the Palais-Royal in the aftermath of the Revolution of 1848. On April 29, 1851 Siboutie wrote.

"I have been to the Palais-Royal to see the exhibition of Gobelins, Sèvres, and Beauvais. The handiwork of our artists is indeed beautiful. The exhibition is installed in the apartments of Louis-Philippe and his family. My heart ached at the site of the traces of the Revolution of 1848. None of the damage done then has been repaired. The marks of bullets and bayonets are still on walls, paneling, and marble pavements; mirror and picture frames hang empty, gilding has been defaced, evidences of unreasoning fury and vandalism offend the eye everywhere. I reflected sadly, as I walked through the exhibition, that had it been held on February 24, 1848, its priceless treasures would have met a like fate." (10)

Sixteen films and numerous television shows have used the Palais-Royal as a stage set. Remember when Cary Grant was shooting it out with Walter Matthau, while Audrey Hepburn looks on in the 1963 classic thriller Charade? The columns each of them hid behind are beside the gardens of the Palais-Royal.

June 1815: France takes revenge for the Battle of Waterloo at the Palais-Royal.

June 18, 1815 was a bitter moment in French history with Napoleon's defeat at Waterloo. Prussian soldiers were encamped at Montmartre, Scottish highlanders lived along the Champs Elysées, the Palace Vendôme hosted the Russian general staff, and the Austrians were occupying the Champs du Mars.

Parisians took their revenge on the occupying armies at the gambling houses of the Palais-Royal. At the Café Borel, General Blücher, the Prussian field marshal and hero of Waterloo, lost in a single evening, a million and a half francs. Between the gambling losses, cheap champagne, and expensive ladies of the evening, the Palais-Royal and its gardens extracted a steep price for hosting the victorious allies.

1815: Galignani's New Paris Guide or Stranger's Companion

In 1815 Giovanni Antonio Galignani was making a living teaching English and Italian in Paris, when Napoleon Bonaparte lost the Battle of Waterloo to English, Russian, and Prussian armies. An enterprising businessman Galignani publishes for the first time, what was to become a classic in the annals of tourist literature, *Galignani's New Paris Guide* for English and German speaking visitors. A bilingual book with the English language on the left page and the German text on the right page, the book was designed to sell to occupying soldiers from England and Prussia. Various editions are still available through the Firm Galignani.

Let us go back two centuries and read of the Palais-Royal Gardens, as if we were one of the Duke of Wellington's soldier-tourists. The guide indicates that the original garden in Cardinal Richelieu's time was a parallelogram of 1000 feet by 432 feet, filled with chestnut trees all trained to shape by iron bands. Galignani recounts how the tri-colored cockade from the Revolution originated in the garden. Shopping in the galleries will be expensive, but the variety is considerable including jewelry, watches, furniture, tailors, milliners, perfumeries, and moneychangers. Galignani recommends several restaurants including the Very, Véfour, Café de Foy, and the Trois Fréres Provençaux. Scams abounded. Galignani warned of fake auctions where customers are lured into paying exorbitant prices for merchandise. Beware of pickpockets looking to steal your watch and cash. Then as now there were chairs and benches all through the gardens for strollers. In 1801 Galignani established Europe's first English language bookstore in Paris. This delightful establishment still thrives on the Rue de Rivoli.

1878: George Augustus Sala writing in the London Daily telegraph

The popular columnist George Sala had witty observations strolling through the gardens of the Palais-Royal in 1878. Sala noted that the arcades were not as popular as in decades past, but the gardens were still a decent place to waste an afternoon. Similar to visitors today Sala wondered at all the people who had the spare time to idle away an afternoon.

Galignani's bookstore on the Rue de Rivoli

Sala described a visit to his favorite shop, the Galerie d'Orléans, owned by M. L. Desbords. Monsieur Desbords was recognized for his porcelain pigs portraying a Monsieur Pig in all aspects of the human condition. Examples were Monsieur Pig being drunk, suffering from a headache, being beaten by his wife, and having an argument with his mother-in-law.

In August 1914 at the start of World War One American expatriates were unable to join the French Foreign Legion until French reservists had been called up and placed in their units. Answering the call a few Americans living in Paris decided to form a volunteer militia named the American Volunteer Corps. One of the stores in the Palais-Royal offered to become the local recruitment office, while the enlisted men drilled in the garden. Nothing developed from the cause and when the Foreign Legion opened to enlistments, the organization disappeared.

August 24, 1944: The day before the liberation of Paris, the Comédie Français becomes a hospital and weapons cache for the Resistance.

During World War Two and the German occupation of Paris, the Comédie Français Theater beside the Palais-Royal gardens was a Resistance center. Weapons were kept in the downstairs boiler room. When the shooting started on August 24, 1944, the House of Molière became a hospital. Actresses Marie Bell, Lise Delamare, and Mony Dalmès became nurses.

August 11, 1954: Funeral of Sidonie Gabrielle Colette

The invitation simply stated, The Funeral of Colette. It was the first time in the history of the four French republics a woman had received a state funeral. The service was held at the end of the Palais-Royal's garden opposite to the end where Colette had lived most of her life. Having died just the night before, Colette was placed in a casket draped with the Grand Cross of a Chevalier and Grand Officer of the Legion of Honor. Pots of blue gladioli filled the garden as blue was Colette's favorite color. Colette always wrote on blue paper.

Sidonie Garbielle Colette, one of France's greatest writers, had lived first at 9 Rue de Beaujolais on second floor from 1927 to 1929. The apartment was located just at the end of the Palais-Royal garden. In 1938 she moved to the first floor and spent the rest of her life there. Most English-speaking readers are familiar with Colette's two novels *Chéri* (1920) and *Gigi* (1945), both made into successful films.

Colette's writings in *Paris from My Window* (*Paris de ma fenêtre*), published in 1944, recounted daily observations and thoughts at her apartment in the Palais-Royal during the Nazi occupation.

Here are two of the more well-known quotes from *Paris de ma fenêtre*.

"The true traveler is he who goes on foot, and even then, he sits down a lot of the time." (11)
"To a poet, silence is an acceptable response, even a flattering one." (12)
During the whole of the German occupation Colette hid her Jewish husband, Maurice Goudeket, in their apartment.

Plaque commemorating Colette's life at the Palais-Royal

1986: Abstract minimalist Daniel Buren installs the Les Deux Plateaux into the Palais-Royal Court of Honor.

How does a two-thousand-year-old Paris assimilate modern art? Occasionally this accommodation has been controversial, as was the case with what are called Buren's Columns. In 1985, the Court of Honor in the Palais-Royal was a parking lot for employees of the Ministry of Culture. Culture minister Jack Lang commissioned Buren to create an installation in the courtyard to beautify the area and cover the ventilation shafts for the surrounding edifices. Completed in 1986 the installation immediately elicited debate. Criticized for its cost, city fathers believed the creation integrated poorly with the surrounding architecture. Utilizing his signature stripped themes; the array of columns was recently renovated.

Les Deux Plateaux by Daniel Buren in the Court of Honor Palais-Royal (the little boy above is insisting his mother stop along their walk and play with his handful of toy cars. Mother played along.)

How to get there: Use métro station Palais-Royale-Musée du Louvre. If you are walking, the Palais-Royal complex is situated on Rue Saint Honoré.

The neighborhood originates from Roman times. When building the first basins centuries ago, medallions of the emperors Diocletian and Valentinian were excavated from beneath the Palais-Royal garden. Today France's Constitutional Council and the Ministry of Culture occupy most of the space in the Palais-Royal buildings. Parisians and visitors alike enjoy world class shopping along the Rue Saint Honoré and the Place Vendôme. Besides the Palais-Royal gardens the first arrondissement features the history laden Jardin du Tuileries, Square del la Place Dauphine, and Square du Vert Galant.

Chapter 2. Jardin des Tuileries

"The word impossible is not French." (1) Napoleon Bonaparte (1769–1821)

The Tuileries Garden began with a mother's obsession with her two sons. When the mother was Catherine de Medici, Queen Regent of France and the two sons were Charles IX and Henry III, the future kings of France, the pot got stirred. What began as a muddy strip of land along the Seine in the 13th century became home to a series of tile factories or kilns (*tuileries*). The Duchess of Angoulême, mother of Francis I, wished to live on the shoreline, whereupon Francis purchased the land for a villa. During the reign of Charles IX, Charles and Henry were living in the Louvre, the old medieval palace of the kings. Catherine, living in the Hôtel des Tournelles, decided to build a new palace for herself. The over protecting mother and domineering Regent ensured that the new palace was near her sons' apartments in the Louvre to keep a watchful eye on events. Catherine's Renaissance palace, soon to be known as the Tuileries Palace, was completed in 1572.

Catherine wished the garden of the palace to capture the look of the parks in her native Florence. She commissioned Bernard de Carnese, a Florentine landscape architect, to create an Italian Renaissance garden on the front steps of the Palace. The Tuileries Garden was born. In 1667 Charles Perrault, a favorite of Louis XIV and author of *Little Red Riding Hood*, *Puss in Boots*, *Cinderella*, and *Sleeping Beauty*, asked Louis to make the Tuileries Garden accessible to the public. Louis agreed and the Tuileries Garden became the first royal park in Paris available to Parisians. A city ordinance forbade soldiers and beggars from entering. Today a stroll through the Tuileries offers vestiges of the park's late Renaissance beginnings.

Tuileries Garden

June 5–6, 1662: "The queen has a boy!" The king gets a mistress.

On November 1, 1661 at the Château de Fontainebleau, Louis XIV witnessed the birth of his first son the Grand Dauphin, Louis of France. Louis was said to have run to the window and shouted to the awaiting court below, "The queen has a boy!" Seven months later Louis celebrated his son's birth with a two-day spectacle in the Tuileries Garden. However, those royals living in the inner circle at court knew well the true reason behind the festival which became known as *Le Grand Carrousel*. At this time the twenty-four-year-old Louis was falling in love with eighteen-year-old Louise de La Vallière, a maid of honor to Princess Henrietta, Anne of England. Princess Henrietta, nicknamed *Minett*, was living at Fontainebleau with her husband Philippe of

29

France, the King's brother. Together they were known as Monsieur and Madame given their rank at court. Louis began showing an interest in Henrietta, which created a potential international scandal, given Henrietta's nationality and her being Louis's sister-in-law. The two contrived to divert peoples' attention by Louis outwardly showing interest in someone else. This someone else was the pretty and charming Louise. Louis promptly fell in love with Madame La Valliére and forgot Henrietta. *Le Grand Carrousel*, celebrating the birth of his son, was a perfect excuse for Louis and Louise to enjoy a weekend fit for the Sun King.

Le Grand Carrousel was a history-making event commemorated on stamps and captured on canvas. The creative Charles Perrault choreographed part of the spectacle as a *carrousel*, a popular military drill, where four horsemen performed special square-shaped formations or designs, a quadrille. The exact routines performed by the participants are unknown today, but we know that the king and his entourage took part in the festivities. The first quadrille's Roman theme featured horsemen dressed as Roman legionnaires, drummers, and trumpeters. Louis led the procession dressed as an emperor followed by his senators. The King's brother, Phillipe, Henrietta's husband, led a procession as a Persian king, while the Duke de Condé portrayed an Indian prince. The last event featured the Duke de Guise leading a group of riders dressed as American Indians. Today the location retains the name Place du Carrousel.

France's fabulist La Fontaine, attending the event, took a cynical view on this gaudy display by the aristocracy and wrote:

> But the nobility
> Could not go in so free,
> Who proudly had assumed
> Each one a helmet plumed;
> We know not, truly, whether
> For honor's sake the feather,
> Or foes to strike with terror; (2)

La Fontaine's words were prophetic for the seven lines are taken from his fable *The Battle of the Rats and the Weasels*. Once there was a battle between the Rats and the Weasels. The Rats turned the tide and began to annihilate the Weasels. However, the saving grace for many Weasels were their ability to squeeze themselves into all shapes of holes and crevices and thus escape death. But the Weasel nobility wore large plumed helmets as a show of rank and prestige. The nobles' helmets prevented them from escaping death to the Rats.

Carousel in Paris

Englishman Martin Lister, in his travelogue, A Journey to Paris in the Year 1698, heartily recommended the Tuileries Garden as a wonderful place to sit and enjoy an afternoon, especially along the shaded banks on either side of the park. Unlike today, the Tuileries Garden was full of wildlife including songbirds, rabbits and partridges. His favorite spot was called the Amphitheater of the Hedges, which included a stage and spectator seats for concerts.

May 30, 1770: Tragedy mars the royal wedding celebration of Louis XVI and Marie-Antoinette.

A display of fireworks was planned to start the celebrations in the Tuileries Garden and along the Seine to commemorate the wedding of the Dauphin, the future Louis XVI, and the Archduchess Marie-Antoinette of Austria. The fireworks prematurely exploded on the ground, causing a panic. One hundred and thirty-three Parisians died and another three hundred spectators were severely injured.

In his memoirs the Count of Tournell spoke of his pleasant strolls through the Tuileries Garden in 1725. However, young couples having sex up against the trees in the evening shocked the Count.

1774–1784: Double agent, Dr. Edward Bancroft passes secrets in the Tuileries.

In 1774 Dr. Edward Bancroft was a physician studying in London and a colonial representative of Connecticut for trade opportunities. Benjamin Franklin, already stationed in London representing Pennsylvania, met Bancroft and became friends. Franklin hired Bancroft as a spy and member of the American colonies' Committee of Secret Correspondence. In June 1776 Silas Deane, Bancroft's old medical professor, already a spy for the colonies, arrived in England. Deane's overt reason for being in England again was trade, but his real purpose was to obtain French assistance for the Americans' coming war with England. Bancroft worked for Deane as an interpreter and reported to Deane as a spy. However, watching events unfold Bancroft became alarmed at the impending prospect of war with England and involvement with the French.

Against total American independence Bancroft decided to help the British. Paul Wentworth, recently hired by the British Secret Service, introduced

Bancroft to Lords Suffolk and Weymouth, directors of the Service. They convinced Bancroft to become a British double agent. Luckily for Bancroft Franklin had just appointed him as secretary to the American Commission in Paris, allowing Bancroft access to privileged information. Bancroft wrote a weekly letter to a Mr. Richards from a Mr. Edward bragging about his love life. In between the text, in invisible ink, Bancroft reported to the British Secret Service.

Entrance to the Tuileries Garden at the Place de la Concorde

Each Tuesday evening Bancroft took a walk in the Tuileries and placed the letter in a small glass bottle, hidden in the trunk of a box tree along a path. A British agent took the letter and replaced the bottle with new instructions for Bancroft, which was retrieved later in the evening. Rumor suggested that George III learned of the French-American Treaty of Alliance two days after its signing. Bancroft was never caught.

Over a century later in 1891, the British government declassified files which revealed Bancroft's role as a double agent. After the Americans won independence Bancroft remained in England, became a wealthy businessman, and was surprisingly made a foreign honorary member of the American Academy of Arts and Sciences.

A walking path through the Tuileries Garden

December 1, 1783: The first manned flight of a hydrogen balloon leaves the Tuileries Garden.

On December 1, 1783 Jacques Charles and Nicolas-Louis Robert piloted the first manned hydrogen balloon flight over Paris ascending to an altitude of 1,800 feet and landing in the village of Nesles-la-Vallée two hours and five minutes later. The trip covered near thirty-six kilometers. Louis-Sébastien Mercier, a spectator, wrote in his popular travelogue, *Le Tableau de Paris*, that two hundred thousand Parisians were on hand for the event and crowded into the Tuileries Garden on a perfect sunny day. Mercier related how the crowd feared for the two men and admired their courage. Those paying a one-crown fee to help finance the venture got a preferred spot to watch the launch. A special guest was the United States Ambassador to France, Benjamin Franklin. Today a plaque commemorates the flight in the Tuileries Garden. Ten days earlier on November 21, 1783 the Montgolfier brothers achieved the first human flight in a hot air balloon as opposed to a hydrogen-filled balloon. Ambassador Franklin also watched that first flight.

Plaque commemorating the first hydrogen balloon flight

Friday, August 10, 1792: Sans-culottes amass in the Tuileries Garden and storm the Tuileries Palace.

The *sans-culottes* of the Paris Commune rioted on this Friday in the Tuileries Garden and attacked the Tuileries Palace. *Sans-culottes* were named because French peasants wore inexpensive pants (pantaloons) in place of the expensive silk knee breeches, *culottes*, worn by the nobility. Working class Parisians were fed up with the spoils of the Revolution going solely to the property owners and professionals. Louis XVI and his family fled to the nearby Legislative Assembly building, when the crowd slaughtered at least 700 Swiss guards defending the palace. The corpses were stripped of their clothes and piled high in the area in front of the palace at the Place du Carrousel. Other bodies were thrown haphazard throughout the garden and along the banks of the Seine.

August 21, 1792: French revolutionaries erect a guillotine at the Place du Carrousel.

One-hundred-thirty years after hosting Louis XIV's Grand Carrousel, the Place du Carrousel now accommodated a guillotine where it remained until May 11, 1793. Thirty-five French were executed. On August 2, 1793 the government built a wooden memorial on the Place to honor Jean-Paul Marat, the revolutionary journalist murdered by Charlotte Corday.

January 21, 1793: Louis XVI is guillotined at the Place de la Révolution

Place Louis XV, built in 1755 as a continuation to the Tuileries Garden, featured statuary and fountains to honor Louis XV. A large equestrian statue of the king featured prominently in the center of the square. In 1793 the square was renamed the Place de la Revolution. The equestrian statue was destroyed. The Convention had already convicted Louis XVI of treason, and now on January 21, 1793 Louis was guillotined. In the years to follow many others were to die here including Queen Marie-Antoinette, the chemist Antoine Lavoisier, and revolutionary hero Maximilien Robespierre.

In 1795 the Directory government renamed the large square the Place de la Concorde. The Bourbon Restoration government changed the name back to the Place Louis XV in 1815. During the reign of Charles X, the name changed again in 1826 to Place Louis XVI. In 1830, after the overthrow of Charles X, the new government of King Louis-Philippe changed the name back again to the Place del la Concorde.

Charles-Henri Sanson performed the execution of Louis XVI as High Executioner of the First Republic. Prior to the Revolution Sanson was a fourth-generation executioner under the monarchy. Sanson began studying medicine for a career, but when his father's health failed, Sanson assumed his father's hereditary position. Sanson executed 2,918 victims over a forty-year career. Charles enjoyed playing the violin and cello, and attending the operas of Christoph Gluck.

August 9, 1803: Robert Fulton tests the first steamboat beside the Tuileries Garden.

It was an action-packed journey for Renaissance man Robert Fulton before testing his steamboat alongside the Tuileries Garden in the Seine.

Already a successful portrait painter having studied under Benjamin West, Fulton possessed a long-term interest in marine engineering. Fearing limited opportunities in America, Fulton moved to France in 1788, where he initially developed the submarine Nautilus, in hopes of selling the warship to France for the war with England. After construction in Rouen, Fulton completed several successful dives in the Seine lasting up to four hours and achieving depths in excess of twenty feet. The French Admiralty were skeptical of its usefulness even after sinking a small sloop provided by the French Navy. At the same time Robert Livingston, U. S. Ambassador to France, encouraged Fulton's interest in steamboats.

Livingston arranged for several Parisian businessmen to finance the building of the boat in Paris. Fulton's first design was a failure. When the steam engine and boiler were lowered into the hull, the frame straightaway broke apart and the boat sank. After strengthening the hull, the new boat had a length of sixty-six feet, and an eight-foot beam. On August 9, 1803 the boat powered up and down the Seine in front of the Tuileries Garden reaching speeds of three to four miles per hour against the current.

Place del la Concorde

Despite the apparent success, Fulton was unable to convince the French to sponsor further development. Fulton left for England with hopes of convincing the English Navy to develop marine torpedoes in 1804. He achieved negligible success against the French at the Battle of Boulogne. Admiral Nelson's victory at Trafalgar ended English interest, providing Fulton with an excuse to return to America, where fame awaited in the commercial development of the steamboat. Some sources claim that Fulton's nickname was "Toot"!

1840: The Paris Sketch Book of Mr. M. A. Titmarsh

In the 19th century, when wealthy English were making the Grand Tour of Europe, strolls through the Tuileries Garden were particularly enjoyed. Many of those visitors stayed at the fabled Hotel Meurice, founded in 1815, which looks out over the park.

William Makepeace Thackeray, author of *Vanity Fair*, and writing under the pen name of Michael Angelo Titmarsh wrote *The Paris Sketch Book* in 1840, where he offers endless observations by the opinionated Mr. Titmarsh on an Englishman's experiences in the City of Light. Titmarsh comments with great humor on every facet of French culture and history. An early observation focused on where to stay in Paris.

"And now, if you are a stranger in Paris, listen to the words of Titmarsh. – If you cannot speak a syllable of French, and love English comfort, clean rooms, breakfasts, and waiters; if you would have plentiful dinners, and not particular (as how should you be?) concerning wine; if, in this foreign country, you will have your English companions, your porter, your friend, and your brandy-and-water – do not listen to any of these commissioner fellows, but with your best English accent, shout out boldly, 'Meurice!' and straightaway a man will step forward to conduct you to the Rue de Rivoli." (5)

In 1835 owner Charles-Augustin Meurice moved the hotel from its original location at 223 Rue Saint Honoré to its present location overlooking the Tuileries. Having an English-speaking staff, the Hôtel Meurice advertised, "For an English traveler, no hotel in Paris offers more benefits than Le Meurice." (3)

February 24, 1848: Louis-Philippe I, the last King of France

Albert Vandam was a small boy when he witnessed the fall of the King of France in 1848. Many decades later as a journalist Vandam relived this childhood memory. Standing in the Tuileries Garden amongst a huge crowd Vandam witnessed thousands of National Guardsmen confronting regular French army soldiers in front of the Tuileries Palace. Shots had already been exchanged. Vandam watched Louis-Phillipe I, in a Guardsman uniform, ride to the front of the National Guard between the two forces. Several troops shouted "Vive le roi!" but the vast majority countered with "Vive le

Réforme!" Knowing his support had vanished Louis-Phillipe abdicated. The monarchy in France ended and the Second Republic began.

Location and plaque of the Fulton's experiment of August 9, 1803.

May 23, 1871: Paris Communards burn the Tuileries Palace to the ground.

After the defeat of the Second Empire during the Franco-Prussian War in September 1870, the Third Republic was proclaimed with Adolphe Thiers as the chief executive. The Republic continued the war with Prussia with disastrous results. From September 1870 through January 1871 the Prussian army surrounded and laid siege to Paris. During this period radical revolutionaries, named the Commune, formed their own government in Paris and challenged the legitimacy of the Republic.

Hotel Meurice on the Rue de Rivoli

On May 15 the World's Fair of 1855 opened in Paris. For the first time, visitors to Paris saw those famous words sitting in shop windows beside the Tuileries Garden, "English spoken here."

On February 24, 1871 the Republic signed a peace agreement and surrendered to Prussia ending the war. The Commune continued its revolutionary fight by refusing to recognize the Republic as the legitimate government of France. Based in Versailles, the Thiers government, sent an army to Paris to crush the Commune rebels. During the last stages of the revolt, Jules Bergeret, commander of the Commune, ordered twelve men to set fire to the Tuileries Palace, a symbol of the Second Empire. Using turpentine, oil, and explosives, Communards watched the palace burn for forty-eight hours leaving a charred shell next to the Tuileries Garden. In 1882 the French National Assembly voted to demolish the palace ruins and completed the demolition in 1883.

April 21, 1878: The Legend of the Phantom of the Tuileries Palace—the Little Red Man

George Augustus Sala began his journalistic career working for his friend Charles Dickens writing features in Dickens's *Household Words*. Writing for the London Daily Telegraph Sala became one of Europe's most popular journalists. His writings covered every conceivable subject in a pompous, opinionated, and witty style. Sala's story, *The Little Red Man*, brought French folklore to the Tuileries Garden and Palace.

On the night of April 21, 1878 Sala saw the *Diable Boiteux* (limping Devil) dressed in red, having cloven feet, a humped back, a most infernal grin, one eye, carrying a mandolin, and with a raucous strident voice singing songs of events past. Sala recounted, "As I left and crossed into the Rue de Rivoli, I saw him again in the blackened and charred window frames of the Tuileries Palace, here was the eidolon of Napoleon I famous for entering the emperor's tent the night before the Battle of Austerlitz whispering `St. Helena' into his ear."

According to Sala the Phantom of the Tuileries Palace was first seen in 1792. He was wearing the Phrygian Cap of Liberty with a tricolored cockade, singing the La Marseillaise and chanting, "saints of paradise, pray for Charles X!" And again in 1793 the Phantom sings the Hymn of the Supreme Being, swears allegiance to Robespierre, and chants "saints of paradise: pray for Charles X!" In 1815 the Little Red Man now wears a suit like that of the Marquis de Carabas, dons a 3-corned hat, and has a long pigtail. He is shouting Napoleon is overthrown, long live Henry IV, and chants "saints of paradise: pray for Charles X!"

The legend of the Little Red Man is much older. Our saga began in the year 1565. Catherine de Médici, recent widow of Henry II of France, was living in the Hôtel des Tournelles and wanted to live closer to her son, Charles IX. She bought up several old kiln factories along the Seine next to the Louvre

Palace forcing out the local businesses and homes. Included in the group was, Jean the Flayer, a butcher who refused to leave. Rumors related that Jean was murdered because he had a loose tongue regarding Catherine's political intentions or that he was the Queen's own henchman who ran afoul of his patron. Either way he was slain, and at the moment of his death, vowed revenge and his return. The Phantom disappeared until 1571 when, during construction of the Tuileries Palace, Queen Catherine and her court astrologer, Cosimo Ruggieri, both witnessed the Little Red Man. The Phantom reappeared many times and taunted Catherine until her death on January 5, 1589. Decades later he was thought to have appeared at the Palace foretelling the assassination of Henry IV, and to have foretold and appeared at the death of Louis XIV. When rioters chased Louis XVI and Marie-Antoinette into the Tuileries Palace where they remained under house arrest, his ghost allegedly appeared to Marie on several occasions. The Queen sought help from the well-known occultist, Robert-Francois Quesnay de Saint Germain, but without success. The Little Red Man haunted the Queen until her death in 1793. Parisians were said to have seen him in a palace window, when Communard rebels burned the Tuileries Palace to the ground in 1871.

May–November 1878: Henry Giffard's balloon ride at the 1878 Paris World's Fair

A star attraction at the Paris World's Fair of 1878 was inventor Henry Giffard's balloon ride located in the center of the Tuileries Garden. Having a volume of 25,000 cubic meters the mega balloon carried up to fifty passengers at a time to a height of fifteen hundred feet. Operated like any other amusement ride the balloon completed ten ascents per day. Giffard located a hydrogen generator right alongside the tethered balloon and gave free small balloons to passengers as souvenirs.

Famed actress Sarah Bernhart rode with the inventor. Taken with the experience, Bernhart commissioned Giffard to build a custom untethered balloon she named the Dona Sol. Leaving the Tuileries, she landed at the train station in the nearby village of Emerainville. During the trip Sarah and her passengers enjoyed a lunch consisting of bread, foi gras, oranges, and champagne.

June 13–July 3, 1898: The first Paris Motor Show is held in the Tuileries Garden.

Twenty-five hundred square meters were set aside for this premier automobile event in the Tuileries. Co-founder, the Marquis Jules de Dion, brought two hundred manufacturers together to display over 232 different models. The event was a huge success and continues to the present as a biennial event at the Paris Expo Porte de Versailles. Jules de Dion was more than a successful businessman and won the first automobile race in the world. Held on July 22, 1894 the race began in Rouen and ended in Paris, a distance of seventy-six miles. Analogous to a handful of automobile races today, the winner de Dion was disqualified for rules infractions.

March–August 1918: The Germans terrorize Paris.

They were the first man-made objects to reach the stratosphere. Parisians thought they were from a high-altitude Zeppelin. Witnesses in the Tuileries Garden stated that the craters left in the park were about ten to twelve feet in diameter and four feet deep. The first explosion took place at 7:18 a.m., March 21, 1918, next to the park on the Quai de la Seine. After enough fragments were collected, the French understood the Germans had deployed a new gun that fired shells, not aerial bombs. Days later Didier Daurat, a French air reconnaissance pilot, located what is now known as the Paris Gun (*Paris-Geschütz*). The Paris Gun was the largest artillery piece of World War One, firing a 234-pound shell up to eighty-one miles.

Military historian Adam Hochschild wrote that it took approximately three minutes for each giant shell to reach Paris climbing to an altitude of twenty-six miles, a summit not reached again until October 1942, when the German V-2 rocket achieved such heights. Gunners, in calculating where the shells landed, had to adjust for the rotation of the Earth (Coriolus Effect). A total of seven guns were built, brought by rail, and implanted into concrete at Coucy-le-Château-Auffrique outside Paris. Up to 367 shells were fired into Paris at a rate of about twenty per day. The shelling killed 250 Parisians and wounded another 620. When the Germans were retreating, they completely destroyed the guns. After the war ended the plans for building the guns disappeared.

The Tuileries Garden hosted fencing at the 1900 Summer Olympics. Featuring epée, foil, and saber, a total of 260 fencers from nineteen nations participated. France dominated all the events with only Cuba, Austria, and Italy winning any remaining medals. Other demonstrations or unofficial events included kite flying, motorcycle and automobile racing, tug-of-war, pigeon racing, ballooning, and firefighting.

11:00 a.m., November 11, 1918: Armistice Day World War One

Americans Helen and Herbert Gibbons lived in Paris throughout World War One and experienced Armistice Day in the Tuileries Garden. That autumn morning, they watched French children climbing and playing over war trophies consisting of captured German tanks and cannons.

As a visitor to this famous garden, one becomes aware that for Parisians the Tuileries is their neighborhood park. One sunny morning I watched with interest, a grade school teacher having his students, about eight to ten years old, running laps around the pond during a gym class.

May 17, 1927: The Musée de l'Orangerie debuts Claude Monet's Water Lilies (Nymphéas) in the Tuileries Garden.

In 1920 impressionist painter Claude Monet offered his services to the French government. Monet wanted to create a series of paintings featuring weeping willows and water lilies to honor the French losses during World War I. Monet's friend, Georges Clémenceau, President of France during the war, suggested that the paintings be housed in the newly renovated Musée de l'Orangerie in the Tuileries Garden. On April 12, 1922, Monet signed a contract donating the paintings to France.

In the following years Monet failed to fulfill the contract, and held onto the works at his home in Giverny until his death on December 5, 1926. Obtaining the paintings after Monet's death, the French government contracted Laurent Fournier, who glued the canvases onto the oval walls in the basement of the museum. The paintings debuted on May 17, 1927.

August 1, 1944: The heroism of Rose Valland

Prior to World War Two the Galerie Nationale du Jeu de Paume in the Tuileries Garden exhibited foreign collections of modern art. At the outbreak of the war in September 1939 the museum's collections were removed to the Chateau Chambord for safety, leaving the museum empty. In 1940 German armies defeated France and occupied Paris until 1944. A "Special Staff for Pictorial Art" (The Reich Leader Rosenberg Institute for the Occupied Territories), or ERR, was sent into France to collect art from France's government museums, private collectors, and galleries. The Jeu de Paume was appropriated to house this collection for its redistribution to Germany. Reichsmarschall Hermann Göring visited the museum no less than twenty times in the next two years to see expositions staged by art dealer Bruno Lohse. Göring left with 594 pieces. The thefts were occurring under the watchful eye of a Rose Valland, an art curator trained at the École nationale des beaux-arts de Lyon.

Beginning in 1940 and lasting until the German departure in 1944, Valland was hired to assist with the sorting and disposition of the more than twenty thousand individual pieces to arrive at the Jeu de Paume. Besides being a member of the Resistance, Rose had made several trips to Germany in the 1920s and 30s acquiring a working knowledge of German. Rose Valland kept detailed records of the arrival of all works, their redistribution to Germany, and where the pieces resided. Valland's meticulous diary was constantly sent to Jacques Jaujard, the Director of the Musées Nationaux and the Resistance. When art was leaving Paris on trains, the Resistance informed the Allies to avoid attacking trains carrying priceless works of art. As the Allies were closing in on Paris Valland learned on the first of August 1944 that the last five boxcars of art were being shipped to Germany. Valland notified Resistance forces resulting in the French Army capturing the train.

The extraordinary efforts and heroism of Rose Valland was the basis for the movie, *The Train*, and for the character of Claire Simone in the film, *The Monument Men*. After the war France awarded Valland the Légion d'honneur and the Médaille de la Résistance, while the United States awarded her the Medal of Freedom in 1948. In 1951 West Germany awarded Valland the Officer's Cross of the Order of Merit of the Federal Republic of Germany.

August 25, 1944: The Allies liberate Paris.

On the morning of August 25, 1944, General Dietrich von Choltitz, commander of the German garrison of Paris, breakfasted with Colonel Hans Jay, his attaché, and subsequently walked in the Tuileries to inspect the troops bivouacked in the garden. Soldiers were just washing up in the ponds. The general remarked to his soldiers that the Parisians were going to have a lovely day for their liberation. At an entry point to the Tuileries the general came upon one of the defending Panther tanks and warned the crew of the coming allies.

In the afternoon Lieutenant Henri Karcher and his company of the Resistance (Forces Françaises de l'Intérieur, FFI) fought down the Rue de Rivoli and through the Tuileries Garden to the Hotel Meurice, headquarters of the German Army. Shooting their way through the hotel lobby, Karcher and his comrades found General von Choltitz, waiting for capture in the hotel dining room overlooking the park. General von Choltitz and his staff were immediately taken to French general Philippe Leclerc de Hautecloque and the Resistance leader, Henri Rol-Tanguy, at the Gare Montparnasse where the general and 17,000 German soldiers officially surrendered.

How to get there: Four metro stops offer easy access into the Tuileries Garden: Louvre-Rivoli, Palais-Royale-Musée du Louvre, Tuileries, and Concorde. The Tuileries Garden is bordered on the north by the Rue de Rivoli and along the Seine by the Quai des Tuileries. The Place de la Concorde and the Place du Carrousel border the west and east ends of the Tuileries respectively.

The Tuileries Garden is located in the first arrondissement, an art lovers delight. The Mona Lisa and the Venus de Milo exemplify the priceless treasures found in the Louvre Museum. The Musée de l'Orangerie and the Musée Jeu de Paume complement the Louvre's vast collections.

While touring the Tuileries Garden consider visiting the Monum Bookstore, dedicated to books on gardening, botany, landscape, and related topics. Many are in English. The store is hidden in a bunker-like edifice at the Place del la Concorde entrance to the Tuileries.

Musée de l'Orangerie

Contract between Claude Monet and the French state where Monet
donated his water lilies paintings to France

Musée Jeu de Paume

Chapter 3. Square du Vert Galant and Pont Neuf

Je me porte comme le Pont-Neuf. This French slang translates
to "fit as a fiddle" or literally, "I carry myself like the Pont Neuf." (1)

Standing on the Pont Neuf and looking down on the Vert Galant park is one of my favorite views of the Seine. Young people often sit along the water's edge bringing food and drink. Men with cane poles try their luck for fish during the summer months. Along the north bank of the park the Vedettes du Pont Neuf are busy taking tourists up and down the Seine. Because the Île del la Cité was the original home of the Celtic Parisii tribe and the future city of Paris, the park and environs have a long and varied history.

The Vert Galant was named after a popular cafe and bathhouse along the Seine, which was swept away in a flood on January 3, 1879. The name of the cafe and the square originates from the nickname given to Henry IV, king of France. Vert Galant, a French slang, equates approximately to what I would term "dirty old man." Henry was a notorious womanizer. Henry even demanded that his second wife, Marie de Medici, raise his illegitimate children with their own offspring. And to complete the portrait Henry was known for a body odor that would drop a horse.

It was here at the tip of Île del la Cité that a Roman emperor was crowned, Vikings pillaged the landscape, Jacques de Molay was burned alive, Henry IV was immortalized, and the artist Christo brought his installation art to the City of Light in the 20th century. Stand in the park below and look up at the level of the bridge. This difference in height, two-plus meters, records the added layers of civilization over the last two thousand years.

Square du Vert Galant and the Pont Neuf

February 360 CE: Julian the Apostate is crowned Emperor of Rome.

In 355 CE the Roman Emperor Constantius II had just completed successful campaigns against the rebellious generals Magnentius and Claudius Sylvanus. The Emperor now required a family member to watch over affairs in the western part of the empire. Summoning his cousin, Flavius Claudius Julianus Augustus, to court in Mediolanum (Milan), Constantius II appointed Julian, Caesar of the West, on November 6, 355 CE. Julian was unprepared for taking command of the western empire. The son of a Roman consul and half-brother of Constantine I, Julian was born and raised Christian in ancient Bithynia and Cappadocia. He had been studying theology under the bishop, George of Cappadocia. Without military or political experience Julian over the next several years became an able military commander with successes against German tribes on both sides of the Rhine.

Julian's problems with Emperor Constantius II began, when the Sassanid Emperor Shapor II invaded Roman Mesopotamia. Constantius II ordered half of Julian's armies to the east for support. Julian's generals, wanting to remain at their homes in Gaul, proclaimed Julian emperor at the Gallo-Roman fortress, where now stands the Pont Neuf and Square du Vert Galant. After another year of campaigning against German tribes, Julian's forthcoming civil war with Constantius II was averted by Constantius's death on November 3, 360 CE. Julian entered Constantinople on December 11, 361 CE as Emperor of the Roman Empire. Although born and raised Christian, Julian reinstated the pagan religions on ascension to the throne, and became the last pagan emperor of Rome, Julian the Apostate.

View down the Seine from the Square du Vert Galant

November 26, 885: The Vikings attack Paris.

When Charles the Fat, King of Germany, Italy, and West Francia, refused to pay tribute to the Norsemen chiefs, Sigfred and Sinric, the Danes at once initiated the largest naval assault ever up the Seine to Paris. Gozlin, the Bishop of Paris, the first of the medieval warrior-bishops, watched from the old Roman ramparts, where the Vert Galant park is today, the approach of nearly 300 Viking long ships, accompanied by an alleged thirty-thousand Norsemen. Refusing again to pay tribute Gozlin and Odo, the Count of Paris, defended the walled Île de la Cité and its two bridges with pitch and hot wax. Gozlin himself was said to have jumped into the battle with bow and axe. After the initial attacks were repulsed, the Vikings laid siege, which lasted until May the following year. Disease killed most of the defenders, including Gozlin, but Odo slipped through the Danish lines and sought help from Charles the Fat. The following October Odo and Charles returned with the imperial army and scattered the Norsemen. Charles encircled Rollo, the last Viking chief on the hill of Montmartre, but let them escape avoiding a bloody confrontation. Odo continued the attacks and prevented the Danes escaping down the Seine; he forced the Norsemen to drag their long boats overland to the Marne River. On Charles the Fat's death in 888, Odo was elected King of West Francia and reigned until his death in 898.

March 18, 1314: Jacques de Molay, the last Grand Master of the Knights Templar, is burned at the stake in the Square du Vert Galant.

Our tale reads like an Alexander Dumas novel. It is the story about the consolidation of power and the accumulation of wealth—politics. The three players are Philip IV, King of France, Pope Clement V, and our victim Jacques de Molay, Grand Master of the Knights Templar.

Philip was in financial difficulty due to the wars with Edward I of England and Edward's allies in Flanders. By 1306 Philip expelled over one hundred thousand Jews from France in order to confiscate their fortunes. King Philip was furthermore heavy in debt to the Templars, who like the Jews, were important bankers and money lenders throughout Europe.

Our second player, Pope Clement V, Raymond Bertrand de Got, owed his papacy to none other than Philip. When Pope Benedict XI died in 1304, Philip coerced the conclave of cardinals to elect Clement to the papacy, although Clement was neither Italian nor a cardinal. Rumors at the time suggested that Clement made a deal with Philip prior to his election resulting in Clement's coronation in Lyon on November 14, 1305. Clement V immediately withdrew the bull, *Unam Sanctam*, which proclaimed papal supremacy over secular rulers. It allowed Philip to go ahead with his plans to charge the Templars with heresy. All types of wild accusations were heaped upon the Templars including sodomy and homosexual practices.

Meanwhile, de Molay, Templar Grand Master and ruler of the island of Cyprus, was working to raise support for a new crusade to the Holy Lands. However, political pressure was building in Europe to unite all the military orders and have a future King of Jerusalem oversee this new united order after Jerusalem was conquered.

In June 1306 Pope Clement summoned de Molay to Poitiers for meetings concerning unification of the religious orders, and to respond to charges of heresy against the Templars. The Grand Master delayed his immediate return, but arrived in France in 1307. In the early morning hours of Friday October 13, 1307 de Molay was arrested with hundreds of other Templars throughout France. The Grand Master was at that moment in Paris attending the funeral of Catherine of Courtenay, sister-in-law of King Philip. Prior to sentencing Jacques de Molay was imprisoned for seven years suffering numerous interrogations by the Church and Philip's officials. Pope Clement completed the arrest of all the Templars in Europe, and Philip realized his goal of confiscating the Templars' immense wealth.

On March 18, 1314, where the small park Vert Galant exists today, Jacques de Molay was finally brought forth for life sentencing. At the last minute he renounced his guilt and decreed his innocence to all charges. Philip, in attendance, was livid, and hastily had de Molay slowly burned to death on the spot without an official trial. De Molay died leaving a martyr's reputation. A brass plaque marks the event on the steps from the Pont Neuf leading into the park. In a remarkable discovery, 687 years later, paleographer Barbara Frale, discovered a copy of the Chinon Parchment which documents Pope Clement's absolution of de Molay and the Templars. The document is dated, August 17 to 20, 1308. The document still resides in the Vatican archives as *Archivum Arcis Armarium D 218.*

Plaque in the Square du Vert Galant observing the execution of Jacques de Molay, Grand Master of the Knights Templar

May 31, 1578: Henry III lays the first stone for the bridge Pont Neuf

It was a rainy Saturday, when Henry III laid the first stone for this new bridge in Paris. Attending were his mother, Catherine de Medici and wife Queen Louise de Vaudémont. Its nickname became *le pont des pleurs* (the bridge of tears), because Henry had just attended the funeral of his friends, Quélus and Maugiron, killed in duels on April 27, 1578. Henry IV opened the bridge after many design revisions in 1607.

1600: A walk across the Pont Neuf

The curator of the Carnavalet Museum of Paris, George Cain, wrote in 1907 regarding his research into life on the Pont Neuf in the mid 1600s. "It was asserted to be impossible to cross the twelve arches of the popular bridge without meeting a monk, a white horse, and two obliging women."

James Bowers

1661: Street life on the Pont Neuf during the seventeenth century

La Ville de Paris en vers burlesques by François Berthaud, was a poetic seventeenth century description of everyday life in Paris including observations on the Pont Neuf and surrounding area, now the Square du Vert Galant.

Square du Vert Galant

O, you Pont-Neuf, rendezvous of charlatans,
Of rascals, of confederates,
Pont-Neuf, customary field
For sellers of paint, both face and wall,
Resort of tooth-pullers,
Of old clo'men, booksellers, pedants,
Of singers of new songs,
Of lovers'go-betweens,
Of cut-purses, of slang-users,
Of masters of dirty trades,
Of quacks and of nostrum makers,
And of spagiric physicians,
Of clever jugglers,
And of chicken venders,
"I've a splendid remedy, monsieur,"
One of them says to you,
"For what ails you…
Look, it smells of sweetest scents,
Is compounded of lively drugs,
And never did Ambroise Paré
Make up a like remedy."
"Here's a pretty song,"
Says another, "for a sou."
"Hi, there, my cloak, you rascal!
Stop thief, Pickpocket." (2)

1782: Having a "brusher-down"on the Pont Neuf

Louis-Sébastien Mercier's, *Le Tableau de Paris* (1782–1788), vividly described street life in Paris just prior to the Revolution. Because the streets of Paris were unpaved, they all became muddy lanes after a rain. A prosperous occupation at the Vert Galant park was the brusher-down. For a small fee a man brushed off your attire, and, if still raining, held an umbrella over you. Mercier further observed, "a fairground, department store, employment exchange, picture gallery, and a poor man's medical center. You could have a tooth pulled out, go through the help wanted, watch tightrope dancers, buy a Lancet or a Fragonard, join the army, pick up the new book by Marivaux or a first edition of Manon Lescaut, arrange to go up in a balloon, watch a bullfight, take fencing lessons, and attend a surgical demonstration."

Paul Lacroix, in his history text, Curiosités de l'histoire du vieux Paris (1858), wrote that Benjamin Franklin had confessed that he never understood the French until spending time amid the street life on the Pont Neuf.

Pedestrians on the Pont Neuf

August 25, 1818: The long and convoluted history of Henry IV's equestrian statue

When Ferdinand, the Grand Duke of Tuscany, died in 1613 he left behind a bronze statue of a horse destined to hold his effigy. Côme II, his heir, inherited the horse and gave it to Marie de Medici when her husband Henry IV died. While being transported, the statue was lost at sea near Sardinia, but recovered. Arriving in Paris, the horse was installed and named, *le cheval de bronze*. In 1635 Louis XIII contracted Italian artists, Giambologna and Pietro Tacca, to create a statue of Henry IV and mount the good King Henry on his horse. By 1788 Henry wore a crown, and in 1789 revolutionaries replaced the crown with a cockade. In 1792 revolutionaries tore the whole thing down and threw it into the Seine.

Henry IV by François-Frédéric Lemot (1771–1827)

After the Restoration in 1818, Louis XVIII contracted François-Frédéric Lemot to create a new statue. Two sculptures of Napoleon were melted down for the occasion, providing the bronze, and the cast was taken from a mold of a surviving cast of the original. A time capsule inside the statue houses a biography of Henry IV, information regarding this second statue, and a list of official sponsors supporting the statue's recreation and installation.

September 22 to October 7, 1985, The Pont Neuf Wrapped

One of several large-scale installations during their career, the artists Christo and Jeanne-Claude wrapped the oldest bridge in Paris, the Pont Neuf, in the fall of 1985. The wrapping consisted of 41,800 square-meters of a sandstone gold colored polyamide fabric. Three hundred workers draped all this "tissue" with 13 kilometers of rope and 12.1 tons of steel cable at each base tower. As with other Christo installations, it created a sensation in Paris during its two-week existence. Christo pronounced that it took greater courage to create ephemeral works when compared to permanent creations.

View down the Seine. Observe the difference in elevation between the street above (far right) and the park below.

How to get there: Use Metro stations Pont-Neuf, Cité, or Châtelet. Visitors staying in central Paris will find Vert Galant within easy walking distance.

Chapter 4. Square Louvois

"Et tu Brute?" (1)
The Tragedy of Julius Caesar by William Shakespeare (1564–1616)

Assassinations have been recorded in history for many millennia. Two examples from classical times are the assassination of Philip II of Macedon, father of Alexander the Great in 336 BCE and Julius Caesar in 44 BCE. Our English word assassin derived from the Middle Latin word, *assassinus*, which is derived from the Arabic word, *Hashshashin*. These Muslim assassins were members of the Ismaili sect during the eleventh and twelfth centuries who were famous for their daring assassinations. Focusing our attention to the lovely little park in the Square Louvois let us turn back the clock to 1820 for one of the more notorious assassinations in French history.

February 13, 1820: The Duke de Berry is assassinated in front of the Théâtre National de la Rue de la Loi.

Believing the Bourbons to be the enemy of France the fervent anti-royal Bonapartist, Louis Pierre Louvel, drove his dagger deep into the chest of Charles Ferdinand d'Artois, Duke de Berry, third child and youngest son of Charles X.

The Duke had just attended a performance of the *Carnaval de Venise* at the Théâtre National de la Rue de la Loi, where the Square Louvois exists today. Nephew of Louis XVIII, the Duke was the last of the Bourbons able to provide a male heir to the family and continue the Bourbon line on the throne of France. Unknown to most, his wife Caroline de Bourbon-Sicilies, at the time of his death, was pregnant. She gave birth to Henri d'Artois seven months later thus perpetuating the Bourbon family.

Square Louvois and the Fountain Louvois by Louis Visconti and sculpture by Jean-Baptiste Klagmann

The assassination of the Duke de Berry was symptomatic of the deep political divisions during the Restoration regime of Louis XVIII. The Seventh Coalition, led by Great Britain and Prussia, had placed Louis on the throne of France against the wishes of most of the French. Both Bonapartists, who wished for a Bonaparte to rule France, and the Republicans, who wanted a return to a democratic republic, hated the Bourbon monarchy.

Like many of the Bourbon family the Duke's life from the Revolution to the Restoration was one of uncertainty and movement. He fled France with his father, the Count d'Artois, and joined the royalist army led by Louis Joseph, the Prince of Condé. The Duke served from 1792 to 1797 distinguishing himself at the Battles of Emmendingen and Schliengen. After a brief time in the Russian army he moved to England where he lived for the next thirteen years.

When Napoleon escaped the island of Elba and returned to claim the throne of France as Emperor, the Duke rejoined the royalist army. As a commander during the Hundred Days War where Napoleon defeated the forces of Louis XVIII, the Duke fled to Ghent when his troops rebelled against him. After Napoleon's defeat at Waterloo during the War of the Seventh Coalition, Louis XVIII reclaimed the throne of France for a second time on July 8, 1815 allowing the Duke to return to France and take his rightful place at the French court.

In September 1824, four years after the Duke's assassination, Louis XVIII died, whereupon the Duke's father Charles Philippe of France (1757–1836), the Count of Artois, and younger brother to Louis XVI and Louis XVIII, became king of France as Charles X. The ultra-royalist Charles X had a stormy relationship with the parliament bringing about the Revolution of 1830, and was forced to abdicate on August 2, 1830. A week later Louis Philippe I took the throne as King of France and was to rule until the Revolution of 1848.

The Théâtre National de la Rue de la Loi was the first theater of that era to have numbered and assigned seats in France.

The current Square Louvois was built in 1830, ten years after the old Théâtre Nationale de la Rue de la roi was torn down. Louis Visconti designed the fountain, and Jean-Baptiste-Jules Klagman created the sculpture representing the four great rivers of France, the Garonne, the Loire, the Seine, and the Saône.

The square's most recent fame occurred in the TV show, Gossip Girl, where the personality Serena (Blake Lively) pushes the character Blair (Leighton Meester) into the fountain at Square Louvois.

How to get there: Use metro stations Bourse or Quatre-Septembre. The Square Louvois is found along the Rue de Richelieu about a block behind the Palais-Royal.

Chapter 5. Square de la Place Dauphine

"And how," asked Louis XIV of a courtier, "do you make love?"
"Sir, I don't make it; I buy it ready-made." (1)
Mercier's *Tableau de Paris* (1782–1788)

If ever there was a park that epitomizes how a small city square in Paris should appear, it is the Square de la Place Dauphine. The street lamps are of the classic candle shape designed by Russian electrical engineer Pavel Yablochkov in 1875. The restaurants are traditional French. Located at the business end of the Île de la Cité and adjacent to the Palais de Justice and the Paris police department, the park primarily hosts nearby workers and residents. Walking here late at night, when the square is empty, is magic.

August 26, 1660: The Joyous Entry of Louis XIV of France and Marie-Thérèse of Spain into Paris on the celebration of their marriage.

Louis XIV created many spectacular public events that earned him the nickname, Louis le Grand; this was one of them, perhaps his first. Having signed the Treaty of the Pyrenees in 1659 ending two decades of war with Spain, Louis brought the countries still closer together with his marriage to Marie-Thérèse, daughter of Philip IV of Spain. Being double first cousins their marriage would be illegal in many countries today. Her father, Philip IV, was brother to Anne of Austria, his mother, while Louis XIII, his father, was brother to her mother Elisabeth of France.

Madame de Motteville witnessed the proxy marriage held at the Isle of Pheasants on the Spanish border. She wrote that the Infanta, Marie-Thérèse, was short, had blue eyes, a fair complexion, and light auburn hair.

This Joyous Entry, a formal ceremonial parade by a monarch exercising his authority over a city, began from the Château de Vincennes outside Paris, and wove its way through seven triumphal arches ending at the Louvre Palace. One of the temporary arches passed into the present Square de la Place Dauphine, where a large amphitheater, hosted an equestrian *carrousel* to entertain the royal entourage. Marie-Thérèse rode in a magnificent carriage drawn by four gray decorated horses, while Louis road beside her on a large bay attired in embroidered robes imbedded with jewels.

View of Place Dauphine looking towards Rue de Harlay

How to get there: Use métro stations Pont-Neuf or Cité. Place Dauphine is located on Île del la Cité in the first arrondissement. One enters the little park from the Pont Neuf through Rue Henri Robert or from the eastern end through Rue de Harlay,

Henry IV started building the Place Dauphine in 1607 naming the area after his son the Dauphine, Louis XIII. This area was the location of the much older Palais de la Cité of the Capetian kings and originally a Roman fortress and palace.

If you stop and relax on one of the park benches in the square, there's a chance you'll be sitting on a bench the actors Yves Montand and Simone Signoret frequented. The couple lived in an apartment facing out over Place Dauphine.

Three famous tourist sites are located on the Île del la Cité: the medieval Sainte Chapelle, the flower market (Le Marché aux Fleurs), and Notre Dame cathedral.

Chapter 6. Square du Temple

"Templar is truly a fearless knight, and secure on every side,
for his soul is protected by the armor of faith,
just as his body is protected by the armor of steel.
He is thus doubly armed and need fear neither demons nor men." (1)
Bernard de Clairvaux 1135

The Square du Temple is a quiet residential park located in the heart of the Haute-Marais neighborhood. The park's main attractions are the exotic collection of trees and the flower gardens containing over two hundred species. Its name derives from the order of the Knights Templar.

1240–1254: The Knights Templar build the Temple fortress in Paris at the present Square du Temple.

After the First Crusade liberated Jerusalem from Muslim control in 1099, the city and surrounding areas became important destinations for Christian pilgrims. The journey was a perilous one. Bandits attacked and sometimes killed whole caravans of pilgrims visiting Jerusalem and other Holy Land sites as they traveled from Mediterranean seaports to inland regions. In 1119 the problem inspired the French nobleman Hugues de Payens to found a militaristic and monastic order having the official name of The Poor Fellow-Soldiers of Christ and of the Temple of Solomon. King Baldwin II of Jerusalem gave them space on the Temple Mount (thought to be the Temple of Solomon), hence the name Knights Templar. The Templars were given official status at the Council of Nablus in January 1120, where they swore to protect and assist the faithful.

By the year 1140 the Templars occupied a large area in Paris centered at the current Place Hotel de Ville along the Seine. In 1240 the Templars expanded their presence in the French capital by buying 140 hectares of land centered on today's Square du Temple. The *enclos du Temple* contained administrative buildings, a chapel, and most impressive, a large keep or donjon fortress nicknamed the Grosse Tour. The Templar complex was completed in 1254. During the next 554 years the Temple fortress was to experience the whims of French history.

Square du Temple at the corner of Rue du Temple and Rue de Bretagne

Friday 13, October 1307: King Philip IV arrests Templar Grand Master Jacques de Molay at the Templar fortress in Paris.

The arrest warrant began with "God is not pleased. We have enemies of the faith in the kingdom." Delivered by King Philip's secret police at dawn on Friday, October 13, 1307 to the Templars in the Temple, the warrant spelled doom for the Templars. For a variety of reasons, though principally financial, (*See* discussion on Jacques de Molay from the Square du Vert Galant) Philip wanted the extermination of the Templars, and with the assistance of Pope Clement V, he accomplished the feat in a most impressive display of efficient cruelty. The Templars confessed to a wide variety of infidelities after lengthy sessions of torture. Knights survived by emigrating to Switzerland or Scotland, converting to other Christian orders such as the Order of Hospitallers, or renaming themselves as they did in Portugal, the Knights of Christ.

Thousands died throughout Europe. Grand Master de Molay, burned at the stake on March 18, 1314 shouted revenge crying, "God knows who is wrong and has sinned. Soon a calamity will occur to those who have condemned us to death." Philip IV and Pope Clement V were both dead within the year.

Friday the thirteenth's ominous reputation has its origin in the arrest of Grand Master de Molay.

1660–1700: Temple gardens hosts evening concerts popular with Parisians.

By the 1600s, Grand Master Jacques de Souvré of the Order of Malta, had transformed the Temple enclosure into a pleasant garden adjacent to the Templar fortress. Chestnut trees shaded the small park, which was opened to the public at the end of the century. Famous writer and memoirist of the age, Roger de Rabutin, related in his family histories the wonderful concerts held in front of the castle fortress. Crystal chandeliers were hung from the trees to light up the evening, while spectators enjoyed La Fontaine, Lully, and Rameau. During the eighteenth century the Temple entertained the likes of Rousseau and Mozart.

When not being caught in a seedy orgy during Holy Week or locked up in the Bastille for his pornographic writings, Roger de Rabutin, Count de Bussy was a cousin and frequent correspondent with Madame de Sévigné the greatest woman of letters during the 17th century (Madame de Sévigné will be discussed in the histories of Place des Vosges). Many fascinating details of the Count's extraordinary life were revealed in his frequent correspondence with Madame. Rabutin's most enduring literary achievement was the novel *Histoire amoureuse des Gaules*, written in 1660. Patterned after *Satyricon*, the satirical novel by Gaius Petronius (27–66 CE), the Count's saucy fiction revealed the lifestyles of many ladies of the court of Louis XIV. The book infuriated Louis and embarrassed several ladies close to the king, which earned the Count a year's stint in the Bastille and permanent banishment from court.

August 10, 1792–January 21, 1793: Revolutionaries imprison Louis XVI and his family in the tower of the Knights Templar.

In June 1792 Louis XVI, Marie-Antoinette, and their children were under house arrest in the Tuileries Palace. Tensions further escalated when on July 28, the Duke of Brunswick, while threatening the borders of France in Coblenz, released the famous manifesto aimed at ending the Revolution. The Duke outraged the revolutionaries by threatening the French with the destruction of Paris by military means, if Louis and his family came to any physical harm and were not immediately restored to full authority in France.

The document stated that the revolutionaries were guilty of treason, and that Paris in particular, will suffer "exemplary and unforgettable acts of vengeance." Seeing they were already guilty, revolutionary leaders felt free to act. On July 29 Maximilien Robespierre demanded that France rid itself of the monarchy. Jean-Paul Marat, on August 9, called for the people to storm the Tuileries Palace and arrest Louis and his family as traitors. Nothing more was to be said. Paris held its breath.

In the early morning hours of August 10, 9,000 of the regional Federation of National Guards, the *Fédérés*, faced off against 900 Swiss mercenaries and another 200 French troops protecting the king. Hoping to defuse the confrontation, the king and his family placed their safety in the hands of the

National Assembly occupying the palace theater, the meeting place of the Assembly. The king stated, "I come here to prevent a great crime."

After being held for three days in the tiny room of the *Logographie* (a small room for reporters watching the Assembly in the old Palace riding academy), the king and his family were taken to the Templar keep, the present location of the Square du Temple. The old Templar citadel, formerly belonging to the king's brother Artois, had been converted into a prison. The insurgent's choice for incarceration couldn't have pleased the French more. It was a dismal, cold, and uncomfortable place. A local newspaper noted with glee that Louis had to climb 126 steps just to get to his third-floor apartments.

The royal family's imprisonment in the Temple was a series of contradictions. The royal family was denied newspapers with no knowledge of the events taking place or the decisions leading to the family's deaths. Yet the Assembly gave Louis thirteen servants for catering and a personal valet. Louis requested and received books. The food was simple, but good. The family was allowed afternoon walks in the fortress courtyard.

Louis's revolutionary guards showed little or no respect for the king and the family. The guards were pranksters, rude, and even cruel. Centuries of built-up hatred by the poor surfaced. It exploded during the September Massacres. On the night of September 3, 1792, when the bloodthirsty street crowds gathered by the Temple, only the tricolor ribbons at the gate of the tower saved the family from being slain. However, the crowd did stick a severed head on a pike through Marie-Antoinette's window. The Temple had become a tourist site in revolutionary Paris with afternoon crowds swelling into the hundreds.

Louis XVI was an accomplished locksmith, and at the time of his death, the most informed geographer in France. He was well read in Latin, French, and English. On January 17, 1792, when learning of his fate to be guillotined, Louis began reading David Hume's History of England (1762) on the death of Charles I.

David Jordan's, The King's Trial: The French Revolution Vs. Louis XVI (2004), offers an intimate account of Louis's imprisonment in the Temple and his trial.

After five months of internal bickering and a complicated trial the Convention found Louis XVI guilty of treason and condemned him to death. At 10:22 a.m. on January 21, 1793 Louis was guillotined at the Place de la Revolution (today the Place de la Concorde) and his body immediately buried at the edge of the city. Ironically, Louis's headless corpse was laid between the 130 Parisians having died in the fireworks explosion in the Tuileries celebrating the King's wedding to Marie-Antoinette and the approximately 600 mutilated bodies of the Swiss guards from the storming of the Tuileries Palace.

Marie-Antoinette was held another six months before being taken to the Concierge prison on the Seine and beheaded on October 16, 1793. The Dauphin, now Louis XVII, died of tuberculosis on June 8, 1795, at the age of ten. His sister, Princess Marie-Thérèse, remained at the tower for three years and four months to the age of eight before being sent into exile. Marie-Thérèse would be the only surviving member of the family after the Reign of Terror.

The next fifty-nine years of Marie-Thérèse's life was like that of a feather riding the winds of European power politics. She first immigrated to Vienna to live with her cousin, Holy Roman Emperor Francis II. Accompanying her uncle, the Count of Provence, the Princess moved to Mitau, Courland, as a guest of Tsar Paul I. In Russia Marie-Thérèse married the Count's son, Louis-Antoine, and immediately moved to Buckinghamshire, England. When Napoleon was defeated in 1815 the Princess could finally return to France as Louis XVIII took the throne. Within months she had to run for it again during the Hundred Days War to Bordeaux. After Napoleon's defeat at Waterloo she returned a second time to Paris under the reign of Charles X, her husband was heir to the throne and she held the title Madame la Dauphine. When Charles X had to abdicate during the Revolution of 1830, she immigrated again to England, ending up in Edinburgh, Scotland. After three years Marie-Thérèse moved to Prague as a guest of her cousin Francis I of Austria. She next moved to the Schloss Frohsdorf near Vienna where she died of pneumonia on October 19, 1851. The Princess was seventy-three years old.

How to get there: Use metro stations Temple or Arts-et-Métiers. The streets Rue du Temple, Rue de Bretagne, Rue Perrée, and Rue Eugène-Spuller enclose the park with the main entrance on Rue du Temple.

By 1808 the Temple had become a place of pilgrimage for royalists; as a result the Emperor Napoleon III ordered the Temple complex's demolition.

The final remnants were demolished in 1857, whereupon Baron Haussmann built the current park and garden. While enjoying the Square, walk down the Rue Eugène-Spuller to visit Le Carreau du Temple, the beautiful iron and glass covered marketplace built in 1863. Restored in 2014 the old clothing market now hosts a variety of events. Enjoy grocery shopping in the Marché des Enfants Rouge the oldest covered market in Paris built in 1628 and situated down the street from the Temple square on the Rue de Bretange. The name "red children" refers to the Hospice des Enfants-Rouges, which closed in 1777. This hospice sheltered children dressed in red clothing, the color of charity.

Pond and gardens in Square du Temple.

Chapter 7. Jardin du Musée Carnavalet

"There is no person who is not dangerous for someone." (1)
Madame de Sévigné (1626–1696)

If you want to learn something about the history of Paris and the Parisians, I can think of no better place than the Musée Carnavalet and the Jardin du Musée Carnavalet. This little museum and its garden, situated in the heart of the Marais, focuses entirely on Paris. Opened in 1880 the Carnavalet's collections span the entire history of Paris from the Roman city of Lutetia through the twenty-first century. The collections are wide-ranging and remarkable. Representative examples are Napoleon Bonaparte's toiletry case and a room recreated with the original furniture where Marcel Proust wrote *In Search of Lost Time*. Jacques des Ligneris, the President of the Parliament of Paris, built the Hôtel Carnavalet in 1548. In 1578, a Breton widow, Francoise Marguerite Kernevenoy, bought the home. Her Breton name, Kernevenoy, translated into French became Carnavalet.

The garden in the Musée de Carnavalet is a classic example of *parterre de broderie*, where the patterns of shrubbery imitate embroidered cloth. Charles VIII brought this Italian Renaissance style to France after his Italian campaigns in 1495. Many of the chateaus in the Loire valley, including the Château de Fontainebleau and the Château de Chenonceau, possess this style of landscape architecture.

The Hôtel Carnavalet was the long-term home of the Marquise de Sévigné. On October 7, 1677 Madame de Sévigné wrote to her daughter, Françoise-Marguerite, on the occasion of her purchase of the Hôtel Carnavalet. Madame de Sévigné lived in the house until her death on April 17, 1696.

"Thank god we have the hotel Carnavalet. It is a good purchase, able to hold all of us, and we will look good; as we cannot have everything, we must forego parquet floors and small fashionable fireplaces; but we will have a beautiful courtyard, a beautiful garden, a beautiful neighborhood." (2)

Madame de Sévigné, herself a Breton, nicknamed the house, *Carnavalette*. Marie de Rabutin-Chantal, marquise de Sévigné, was one of the greatest letter writers in history. Madame's voluminous correspondence with her daughter, the Countess de Grignan, and her cousin, Roger Rabutin, Count de Bussy, offer an intimate portrayal of French society in the seventeenth century. Her letters, portraying court life during the reign of Louis XIV, present a very personal perspective, rarely captured in the historical literature.

"Ingratitude calls forth reproaches as gratitude brings renewed kindnesses."Madame de Sévigné (3)

The following letter to family friend, Madame de Coulanges, written on December 15, 1670, is, besides being often quoted, simply brilliant. The scene was a "guess what" type of gossip. Read it aloud quickly in your best gossipy voice:

"I am going to tell you of an event which is the most astonishing, the most surprising, the most marvelous, the most miraculous, the most magnificent, the most bewildering, the most unheard-of, the most singular, the most extraordinary, the most incredible, the most unexpected, the greatest, the least, the most rare, the most common, the most public, the most private till today, the most brilliant, the most enviable; in short, an event to which there is only one parallel to be found in past ages, and even that not an exact one; an event which we cannot believe in Paris (how then can it be believed in Lyons?); an event which makes everybody exclaim, 'Lord, have mercy upon us!' an event which causes the greatest joy to Madame de Rohan and Madame d'Hauterive; an event, in fact, which will take place on Saturday next, when those who are present will doubt the evidence of their senses; an event which, though it is to happen on Sunday, may perhaps not be accomplished on Monday. I cannot persuade myself to tell you. Guess what it is? I give you three guesses. Do you give it up? Well, then, I must tell you. Monsieur de Lauzun is to be married next Sunday at the Louvre—guess to whom? I give you four guesses,

I give you ten, I give you a hundred. Madame de Coulanges says, 'It is not very difficult to guess, it is Madame de la Vallière.' You are quite wrong, Madame. 'It is Mademoiselle de Retz then.' No, it is not; you are very provincial. 'Dear me, how stupid we are,' you exclaim, 'it is Mademoiselle de Colbert, of course. You are farther off than ever. 'Then it must be Mademoiselle de Créqui. You are no nearer. Well, I find I must tell you. He is to marry on Sunday at the Louvre, with the King's permission, Mademoiselle, Mademoiselle de— Mademoiselle guess the name! He is to marry Mademoiselle, my faith! By my faith! my sworn faith! Mademoiselle, la Grande Mademoiselle; Mademoiselle daughter of the late Monsieur; Mademoiselle granddaughter of Henry IV; Mademoiselle d'Eu, Mademoiselle de Dombes, Mademoiselle de Montpensier, Mademoiselle d'Orleans; Mademoiselle, first cousin to the King; Mademoiselle once destined for the throne; Mademoiselle, the only person in France worthy of Monsieur. Here is a fine subject for conversation. If you cry out, if you are beside yourselves, if you say we are deceiving you, that it is false, that we are laughing at you, that it is a pretty joke, that it is a very poor invention; if, in fact, you abuse us, we shall say you are right, for we have done the same ourselves. Adieu. You will see by the letters you receive by this post whether I am telling you the truth or not." (4)

Saturday, July 25, 1676: A day at the Palace of Versailles

The historical literature sporadically contains eyewitness accounts. On July 29, 1676, Madame de Sévigné, wrote to her good friend the Comtesse de Provence, about her day at one of the most visited tourist sites in the world, the Palace of Versailles. The letter is fascinating in that we get a glimpse of the courtly splendor at Versailles during the life of the Sun King, Louis XIV.

"On Saturday I was at Versailles with Villars, and this is what happened. You know the ceremony of attending the Queen at her toilet, at mass, and at dinner; but there is no longer any necessity for being stifled while their Majesties are at table, for at three o'clock the King and Queen, Monsieur and Mademoiselle, the Princes and Princesses, Madame de Montespan and her train, all the courtiers, all the ladies, in fact, the whole Court of France, go to that fine apartment of the King's which you know. ... A game of *reversis* gives form to the assembly, and settles everything. The King and Madame de Montespan keep a bank together. Monsieur, the Queen, and Madame de Soubise are at one table, Dangeau and Langlée, with their companies, are at other tables. The baize is covered with a thousand louis d'or; they use no other counters. I saw Dangeau play. … He said that I was his partner in the game, and as a result I was seated agreeably and comfortably. I bowed to the King in the way you taught me, and he returned my salutation as politely as if I had been young and pretty. The Queen talked to me a long time about my illness, and she also spoke to me of you. … Madame de Montespan talked to me of Bourbon, and asked me to tell her how I liked Vichy, and whether it did me any good. She said that Bourbon, instead of curing her knee, had given her a pain in both. I saw that her back was very flat, as madame de la Meilleraye had told me; but seriously, her figure is as surprising as her beauty, she is not half so stout as she was, and yet neither her complexion, eyes, nor lips have suffered in the least. Her dress was entirely of French point-lace, her hair was in a thousand curls, and the two from her temples hung very low on the cheeks; her head-dress was composed of black ribbons, intermingled with the valuable pearls that once belonged to the Maréchale de l'Hôpital, some exquisite diamond pendants, and three or four bodkins; in fact, she was a triumphant beauty, and the admiration of all the foreign ambassadors.

This little agreeable confusion without confusion of all the principal people in the kingdom lasted from three o'clock till six. If any couriers arrive, the King retires to read his letters and then returns. Music is played continually, to which he listens, and which has a very good effect. He speaks to those ladies who are accustomed to have that honour. They leave off their game at the hour I mentioned without the trouble of reckoning, because they use no counters or marks, and the pools are of five, six, or seven hundred louis d'or.

At six o'clock they took the air in calèches; the King and Madame de Montespan, Monsieur and Madame de Thianges, who had the good d'Heudicourt upon the box-seat, which to her is a place of paradise. The Queen was in another with the Princesses, and the whole Court followed in different equipages according to their different fancies. They went on the canal in gondolas; where they heard music; they returned at ten for the comedy; at midnight they finished with the media noche; and this is how Saturday passed…" (5)

"Quelle femme aimable! Quell adorable écrivan! Nulle, parmi les femme français, n'a possédé à de degré l'imagination et l'esprit." Saint-Beuve (6)

How to get there: *The closest metro stations to the Musée de Carnavalet are the Hôtel de Ville and St. Paul. The Carnavalet museum is situated on the corner of Rue des Francs Bourgeois and Rue de Sévigné.*

Embroidery patterns in the garden of the Carnavalet Museum

Chapter 8. Square del la tour Saint-Jacques

"I have made this letter longer than usual, only because I have not had the time to make it shorter." (1) Blaise Pascal (1623–1662)

The Square del la tour Saint-Jacques, which surrounds the Tour Saint-Jacques, is a small quiet park along the noisy Rue de Rivoli. Whenever I visit the park only a handful of people are sitting on the benches. The tower is all that remains of the Church of Saint-Jacques-de-la-Boucherie, "Saint James of the butchery", which was destroyed in 1797 during the Revolution. The tower was named a UNESCO World Heritage Site in 1998. Turning back the clock to the fourteenth century we begin with a bizarre tale.

1330-Present: The strange story of Nicolas Flamel

Nicolas Flamel (c.1330–?) was an, *écrivains publics*, a public writer, having two stalls next to the Tour Saint-Jacques. Flamel's shops resided on the old Rue des Écrivains, now the Rue de Rivoli, with many other public writers' stalls. Public writers or scribes offered their services to anyone needing written documents. Flamel was successful during the depressed economic conditions of the Hundred Years War, and continued his success by marrying Perenelle, a wealthy widow of two previous marriages. Together they were generous benefactors to the community, donating funds to the local church, the Church of Saint-Jacques-de-la-Boucherie, and several other church properties in Paris.

Flamel died around 1418, and was buried under the floor of his church, which was torn down centuries later during the Revolution. Flamel and his wife's bones were transferred to the Paris catacombs. The Tower of Saint James alone survived. At this time no knowledge existed of Nicolas Flamel ever having any interest in the mystical pursuit of alchemy, or of authoring any treatises on the subject.

> *The name of the church, Saint-Jacques-de-la-Boucherie, derives from the wealthy Les Halles market butchers who funded the church and the tower. In 950 a small church was built on the location dedicated to Saint-Anne, and in 1340 a second church was erected over the original building. From 1508 to 1522 the current bell tower was built during the reigns of Louis XII and Francis I.*

Flamel's strange celebrity began after his death. The well-known copyist, Guillebert de Mets, noted Flamel's wealth in his, *Description of the City of Paris in 1434*. People believed during the middle ages that persons of common birth acquiring great wealth, possibly obtained their wealth through alchemy, by turning base metals into gold or silver using what was called the Philosopher's Stone. Decades later, rumors appeared hinting that Flamel had acquired the Philosopher's Stone and the power to turn mercury into gold. In the late fifteenth century, a book titled, *The Flower of Flowers* (*Flos Florum*), was attributed to Flamel. In 1561 Robert Duval, mentioned Flamel in his alchemy treatise, naming Flamel as the author of the well-read alchemy essay, *Philosophical Summary*. Paracelsus, the respected German-Swiss philosopher and occultist, gave additional credence to Flamel's authorship of these works.

In 1612 the publication of, *Le Livre des figures hiéroglyphiques* (*The Book of Hieroglyphic Figures*), attributed to Flamel, secured his fame in the world's alchemy literature. The book's success grew with the English version in 1624. The story followed a well-worn plot for alchemy literature. Claimed to have been written around 1400, Flamel began by purchasing an old manuscript for a few coins. Written in Latin, it had the title, *The Book of Abraham the Jew*. The text told of how the author had learned the secret of making the Philosopher's Stone, and therefore, how to turn mercury into gold. Flamel's problem was that the secret was kept in the book's series of hieroglyphs, which were undecipherable. Twenty-one years later Flamel made a pilgrimage to Saint-Jacques de Compostela, where he met with a *conversos*, a Jewish physician. The alchemist-physician told Flamel the secret of how to interpret the hieroglyphs. Flamel described, how beginning with mercury and utilizing the Philosopher's Stone, he produced gold. The book immortalized Flamel.

His fame continued into the nineteenth century with Flamel being mentioned in Victor Hugo's, *Hunchback of Notre Dame* (1831). Flamel's most recent appearance was, as an alchemist in J. K. Rowling's fantasy, *Harry Potter and the Philosopher's Stone* (1998). Dan Brown's novel, *The DaVinci Code* (2003), depicted Nicolas Flamel as one of the Grand Masters of the Priory of Sion. From 2001 to 2010 Flamel was a character in Hiromu Arakawa's manga comic series entitled *Fullmetal Alchemist*, *Assassin's Creed Unity* (2014), an action and adventure video game, set in revolutionary Paris, featured Flamel as an alchemist. Whenever alchemy or alchemists are the subjects of literary endeavors, Nicolas Flamel will no doubt reemerge continuing the unsupported myth.

1648: Blaise Pascal validates theory of atmospheric pressure at the Tour Saint-Jacques.

Blaise Pascal was a rare intellect whose brilliance swept over intellectual disciplines like a glider over a quilted landscape. A few moments of that brilliance were spent in the Tour Saint-Jacques and its gardens. By 1646 Pascal had duplicated Evangelista Torricelli's experiments with a mercury barometer, which led to his study on the effect of altitude on air pressure. Simultaneously, Pascal understood a second phenomenon in the mercury tubes. Pascal's mind was racing ahead of the prevailing Aristotelian dogma, when he concluded that a vacuum was being created at the top of the barometer.

When a mercury tube is turned upside down into a dish of mercury creating a barometer, a space at the top of the tube immediately appears, as the mercury falls. Pascal reasoned that the space was a vacuum. According to Aristotle and the thought of the fifteenth century, a vacuum was impossible. Two years later Pascal's brother-in-law, Florin Périer, performed an experiment on the summit of the volcano Puy-de-Dôme, demonstrating conclusively how air pressure decreased with altitude and how a vacuum was created. Pascal later replicated Périer's experiment in the 50-meter-high Tour Saint-Jacques.

Commemorating the experiment, the city of Paris erected a statue of Pascal next to the tower. These experiments inspired Pascal to invent the hydraulic press and the syringe. The PASCAL programming language is named in Pascal's honor.

Square de la tour Saint–Jacques

Evangelista Torricelli (1608–1647), a student of Galileo Galilei (1564–1642), invented the mercury barometer.

Pascal's genius is equally famous for his literary, philosophical, and theological contributions, besides his discoveries in the fields of physics and mathematics. After his father's death, Pascal turned his attention to religion and philosophy. His first literary achievement was the *Lettres provincials (The Provincial Letters)*, which attacked practices of the Catholic Church. Louis XIV banned the writings as heretical, but their literary achievements were immediately recognized throughout Europe. Pascal's lasting work, published posthumously in 1670, *Thoughts*, is an apology for Christianity. *Pensées* is a large collage of ideas that Pascal never was able to organize and publish, but established Pascal as one of the greatest thinkers of his age.

How to get there: Use metro station Châtelet. The Square del la tour Saint-Jacques is located along the Rue de Rivoli and diagonally situated across from the Place du Châtelet.

The Square de la tour Saint-Jacques occupies the site of the Church of Saint-Jacques-de-la-Boucherie (Church of Saint-James of the butchery), which was torn down just after the Revolution leaving only the bell tower. For centuries pilgrims began at the church the Way of Saint-James, through France, and ending at the Church of Santiago de Compostela in northwest Spain. The apostle Saint-James the Great was buried there. Today pilgrims still make the journey from all over Europe; most still walk.

Starting in 1858, the architect Théodore Ballu completely restored the tower. After being listed as a World Heritage Site by UNESCO, the tower was restored again in 2009. Blaise Pascal's statue resides at the tower's base, and a modern weather station is positioned at the summit,

Le BHV Marais department store sits just two blocks further down the Rue de Rivoli at the metro stop Hôtel de Ville. Located in the basement is one of the more interesting hardware stores on the planet.

Chapter 9. Place des Vosges (Square Louis XIII)

"I will be Chateaubriand or nothing." (1) Victor Hugo (1802–1885)

The Place des Vosges offers neighborhood residents a pleasant city park, an outdoor retreat to sit in the shade or lay out on the lawns and enjoy a sunny afternoon. The arcades surrounding the park offer two additional attractions, a wonderful variety of art galleries and restaurants. Great literature was written here, mortal combats witnessed, extraordinary lives lived, and a great lady of letters was born here. When Henry IV started construction on the Place des Vosges in 1605, this locale had already been the sight of dramatic moments in French history. Since 1388 the Hôtel des Tournelles and its park occupied the site. The Place des Vosges was inaugurated with great fanfare in 1612. Let us begin with the sad death of Henry II.

June 30, 1559: Lord Montgomery's lance mortally wounds Henry II, King of France.

On April 3, 1559, the Peace of Cateau-Cambrésis was signed ending the Italian War of 1551 between France and Holy Roman Empire. Henry II strengthened the agreement with the marriage of his daughter, Elisabeth of Valois, to Philip II, the King of Spain. The two countries had been at war for sixty years, known collectively as the Habsburg-Valois Wars. The marriage aligned the houses of Habsburg and Valois. Although Elisabeth was fourteen years old and Philip thirty-two, the marriage proved to be a good one.

The celebrations included a jousting tournament for the French court. The event was held on the parklands of the old Hôtel de Tournelles, today known as the Place des Vosges or Square Louis XIII. Tragically, during one of the jousts, a fragment of the lance of Lord Montgomery, commander of Henry's Scottish Guards, pierced the helmet of King Henry penetrating his eye and entering the brain. After ten agonizing days Henry died. On his deathbed Henry pardoned Montgomery of any guilt, but Montgomery fled to his estates in Normandy. Horrified of the calamity, Henry's wife, Catherine de Medici, had the palace complex sold as a warehouse for storing ammunition. In 1605 Henry IV began construction of the current Place des Vosges, christening the complex Place Royal.

The earliest recorded joust was in 1099 as an equestrian sport using the heavy cavalry lance. It became popular throughout the Middle Ages, especially in England and Germany. During the reign of Henry II, jousting added a wooden fence separating the riders to prevent collisions. Jousting ended in France after the death of Henry II, but remained popular in the rest of Europe and England. During the reign of Charles VII (1403–1461) the Italian cavalry drill called a *carosello* gradually replaced jousting. The French court embellished the sport into a lavish spectacle having elaborate costumes worn by the riders and their horses. Further development led to ring piercing where riders pierced metal rings with lances while riding legless wooden horses mounted on a rotating wheel. It was immediately popularized into an amusement ride that continues to this day. Carousels were found all throughout Europe by 1800. In America the name merry-go-round replaced the French word *carrousel*. Some merry-go-rounds still challenge riders to grab for brass rings.

April 27, 1578: Duel of the Mignons at Place des Vosges

When visiting the Place des Vosges, most tourists at least stop and look at the entrance to the Musée Hugo, the apartment where Victor Hugo spent many years of his life. Here in the southeast corner of the square, then the grounds of the old Tournelle Palace, one of the most famous duels in French history was fought. At five o' clock in the morning three mignons of King Henry III, Jacques de Caylus, Louis de Maugiron, and Guy d'Arces, paired off against François de Ribérac, Georges de Schomberg, and Charles de Balzac. Caylus, a close personal friend of King Henry, shamed de Balzac over his embarrassing moment with a lady known for her promiscuity. The two quarreled and agreed to duel the next morning. Louis de Maugiron and Guy d'Arces were Caylus's seconds, and François de Ribérac and Georges de Schomberg seconded Balzac. The battle was brief and deadly. Ribérac attempted appeasement, but desired to fight with Maugiron. Ribérac killed Maugiron in the first minutes of the encounter and then died the next day of his own wounds. Guy d'Arces ran his sword straight into the heart of Schomberg, who died instantly, while d'Arces left with a severe head injury. Caylus forgot his dagger, which accompanied a dueler's sword, and paid for it with his life. Caylus left with no less than nineteen deep cuts to his chest and bare arm and died thirty-three days later. Baron Charles de Balzac walked away with minor scratches.

Place des Vosges

April 6-7, 1612: Inauguration of the Place des Vosges

On May 14, 1610 Henry IV was traveling by coach down the Rue de la Ferronerie and got stopped in a seventeenth-century traffic jam. Henry's stopping proved fatal. François Ravaillac, a fanatical Catholic assassin, jumped into the immobile coach and stabbed Henry IV to death, precluding him from seeing the completion of the Place des Vosges. Henry's heir Louis XIII celebrated the opening of the city square with the double wedding of himself to Anne of Austria and the wedding of his sister, the Princess Elisabeth, to the future Philip IV of Spain. More than ten thousand Parisians crowded into the neighborhood to witness 1300 mounted and costumed cavaliers stage an equestrian *carrousel* in the square. Cannons roared from the Bastille and fireworks lit up the night sky surrounding the festivities.

February 6, 1626: Madame de Sévigné is born at the Place des Vosges

On February 6, 1626 Marie de Rabutin-Chantal, the Marquise de Sévigné was born at number 1, Place Royal to Celse Bénigne de Rabutin, the Baron de Chantal, and Marie de Coulanges. Madame de Sévigné became one of the most famous women of letters in French history. Her cousin and close confident, Roger de Rabutin, the Count de Bussy said of her:

"While we are upon this subject, Madame, I must tell you, that I do not believe there is a person in the world who is more generally esteemed than you. You are the delight of mankind. In pagan times, altars would have been raised to you, and you would assuredly have been created the goddess of something or other. In these days we are not so prodigal of incense, above all for living merit, and we content ourselves with saying that you are the most lovely and virtuous woman of your age. I know Princes of the Blood, foreign princes, great noblemen who keep a princely state, great captains, ministers of state, gentlemen, magistrates, and philosophers, who would be your humble servants if you would allow them. What could you desire more?" (2)

May 12, 1627: François Montmorency duels at the Place des Vosges.

François de Montmorency-Bouteville, had already killed the Marquis de Portes in 1625, the Count of Thorigny in 1626, and wounded the Baron Frette in 1627. In May 1627 Guy d'Harcourt challenged the Duke to a duel to avenge the death of his father, the Count of Thorigny.

Plaque commemorating the birth of Madame de Sévigné
at the Place des Vosges

During the duel neither protagonist was injured, but Montmorency's second, François de Rosmadec, killed Harcourt's second, the Marquis de Bussi d'Amboise, ending the duel. This repeated offence against French law carried the death penalty according to an edict decreed by Cardinal Richelieu and signed by Louis XIII in June 1626. Harcourt fled to England to escape prosecution, but Montmorency and Rosmadec were taken prisoner and sent to the Bastille for trial. Montmorency thought Louis and the Cardinal would pardon him, because of his status as a noble. On June 21, 1627, the Parliament of Paris convicted them both and sentenced them to death. Louis was furious at the Duke for his repeated killings and refused to pardon them. Richelieu was to have said to the King, "Sire, it comes to cut the throat to the duels, or to cut the throat of the laws of your Majesty." The following day Montmorency and Rosmadec were beheaded at Place de Greve in front of the Hôtel de Ville.

October 1832: Victor Hugo moves into the Place des Vosges.

In 1832 Victor Hugo and his wife Adele moved to a second-floor apartment at No. 2 Rue de Thorigny in the southeast corner of the Place des Vosges. Hugo lived here until 1848, where he wrote *Marion Delorme*, *Lucrezia Borgia*, *Marie Tudor*, *Littérature et philosophie mêlées*, *La Esmeralda*, *Ruy Blas*, *Les Rayons et les ombres*, *Le Rhin*, *Les Burgraves*, and parts of *Les Misérables*. A host of literary and artistic legends visited Hugo's modest home including Dickens, Lamartine, Gautier, Mérimée, Dumas, and Delacroix. In 1902 French writer Paul Meurice, a close friend of Hugo, instituted the Maison de Victor Hugo as a museum dedicated to the Hugo's memory.

How to get there: Use metro stations Saint Paul, Bastille, or Chemin Vert. If walking from central Paris follow Rue Saint-Antoine going east, turn left (north) onto Rue de Birague, which enters Place des Vosges on its south side.

Place des Vosges, a perfect 140 meters square, was the first planned residential city square in Europe. The architect, Jacques Androuet du Cerceau, designed a uniform red brick building façade, which encompassed the whole square. Henry IV placed a large public garden in the interior space and called the garden the Place Royal. As with other public spaces in Paris, politics altered the name many times. During the Revolution the square was named in succession, Federated Place, Place du artillery, Place of Indivisibility, and ultimately in 1800, Place des Vosges. During the monarchy periods of 1814 to 1830 and 1852 to 1870 the name reverted to Place Royal. The name Place des Vosges returned after the Franco-Prussian War in 1871.

The Place des Vosges was named in honor of the governmental department of Vosges, which was the first regional department to pay its taxes to the new First Republic. The name Vosges originated from the Roman name for the Celtic god of the hunt, Vosegus.

This park inhabits the heart of the Marais neighborhood, which features an amazing variety of attractions. Le Centre Pompidou modern art museum and the Musée National Picasso-Paris are both within easy walking distance. Fashionable boutiques and galleries line many of the small narrow streets. Kosher eateries up and down the Rue des Rosiers offer visitors tasty Jewish cuisine

Hôtel de Ville

Plaque commemorating the home of Victor Hugo

James Bowers

An arcade in the Place des Vosges

Chapter 10. Le Jardin des Arènes de Lutèce

SPQR
Senatvs Popvlvs Qve Romanvs

"Do not trust the horse, Trojans. Whatever it is, I fear the Greeks even
when they bring gifts." (1) *The Aeneid*, Virgil (70 BCE–19 BCE)

Ironically, the Roman arena of Paris, Le Jardin des Arènes de Lutèce,
which held over fifteen thousand screaming spectators in a busy quarter of the
Roman city of Lutetia, now two millennia later, resides in a tranquil domestic
neighborhood. Few tourists are seen in the park. Neighborhood residents and
students from the Université Pierre et Marie Curie campus come here to eat
lunch or just sit and watch children play on the arena floor. What spectators
must have witnessed here two millennia ago!

c. 14–c. 285 CE: Gladiators fight in the Arènes de Lutèce, Paris.

Virtually all Roman cities from antiquity had features considered essential
to cultured life: temples to their gods, aqueducts to provide running water, a
forum to conduct business, a gridded street plan for intelligent town planning,
baths for daily bathing and leisure, a theater for entertainments, and
infamously, an amphitheater for the gladiatorial games. Roman Lutetia
featured all of these, bringing us to the gladiatorial arena in Paris.

Gladiatorial contests originated from human sacrifices honoring the dead
during funeral rites. Rather than sacrificially killing victims at a funeral,
gladiatorial contests added an exciting spectacle to the ceremony. Homer's
epic poem, the *Iliad*, written during the interval of 760–710 BCE, is one of
the oldest written sources of human sacrifices at funerals in western literature.
On the death of the Greek warrior Patroclus his apparition tells his closest
friend Achilles, that he cannot enter Hades without a cremation ceremony
making proper sacrifices to the gods. Achilles sacrificed twelve Trojan

soldiers along with horses and dogs, before placing Patroclus on his funeral pyre. Herodotus in *The Histories*, written c. 450 BCE, wrote of human sacrifices at funerals in Thrace.

The Roman arena in Paris

The Romans inherited the custom of gladiatorial combats from both the Etruscans and the Companians. Sixth-century BCE reliefs in Etruria depict gladiators, known as *bestiarii*, fighting animals in the arena. In 358 BCE the Etruscans slew over three hundred Roman prisoners of war in the forum at Tarquinii. In 264 BCE the funeral of the Roman Brutus Pera was recorded as having three gladiatorial contests. By the Augustan Age in the first century, it was still common for the slaves, who removed the defeated gladiator's corpse, to dress as the Etruscan death-demon Charon. Centuries later the Christian historian Tertullian (c.155–c.240 CE) wrote that the games were offered to placate the dead and to be understood as a funeral rite.

Who were the gladiators? Most came from slavery, as prisoners of war, and perhaps freemen who had fallen on hard times. However, gladiators were, to a degree, the rock stars of the times. Famous gladiators had large groups of followers. Roman citizens even volunteered to fight in the arena. Eventually laws were passed in the Empire banning citizens from fighting. Nonetheless, gladiators were at the bottom of society, ranked equally with actors. Mark Antony's brother, Lucius, fought in the games. The Roman emperors, Caligula, Hadrian, Lucius Verus, and most famously, Commodus, son of Marcus Aurelius, all tried their hand in the ring at staged events portraying themselves as gladiators. Such was the perceived prowess of a gladiator. Uncommonly known today, women too, fought as gladiators. During the reign of Nero, the historian Tacitus wrote about the popularity of female gladiators. As late as 200 CE, the emperor Septimius Severus, passed a law forbidding women to fight at the games.

Returning to our park in Paris, what might Romans have experienced in this arena on a day at the games? Most likely, elected city officials, *duumvirs* or *aediles*, hosted the event. Besides celebrating the death of an important Roman citizen, other civic occasions, such as religious holidays or a victory by Rome's legions, induced gladiatorial spectacles. The most spectacular gladiatorial events in Roman history marked a new emperor's ascension to the throne. Local officials consulted with a *lanistae*, a contractor who hired out gladiators, or a negotiator *familiae gladiatoriae* who made all the arrangements for an event.

When visiting the baths or the forum prior to the games, citizens heard a herald walking through the city advertising the contests. Leaflets would have been posted all over the city proclaiming the games. These posters often listed individual contests between gladiators for devotees who followed the careers of well-known champions. Gladiators owned by the imperial family drew especially large crowds. The day before the games the financiers sponsored a huge feast for the combatants. Besides the gladiators themselves, city fathers, and selected citizens attended.

The day of the games began with the sponsor leading a chariot procession through the streets. Parading gladiators were often attired in the imperial purple robes with gold embroidery. Spectators followed the procession into the arena. The best seating around the arena floor was reserved for male Roman citizens, while the upper rows held the poor, women, and slaves. Seats at the summit of the amphitheater offered scenic views of the Seine and Bièvre rivers, which ran near the Paris arena.

The first contests were bloodless. The contestants, called *paegniarii* or *lusorii*, used wooden swords and spears. Like rock concerts today, these contests were the warm up acts. Trumpets would hush the crowd, and call into the arena the gladiators. Contests would either pit pairs in combat or have small teams fight each other. Occasionally, a team of gladiators was pitted against a group of wild animals such as bears, lions, leopards, or wolves. The spectacle continued all day. References allude to musical accompaniment to the contests in the form of pipe organs, flutes, and singers. Most of the historical literature presents a crowd critical of fighters not performing well or too concerned with their survival. The victors were most often awarded a crown of palm branches, prize money, and continued existence.

At the end of the day spectators would walk out through one of the ground level exits designed to rapidly empty the stadium. In Latin, these architectural structures of an arena were called *vomitoriums*.

Noted historian Michael Grant wrote in his book, Gladiators that some Romans believed drinking the warm blood of a gladiator would cure epilepsy.

How to get there: There are three metro stops within a block of the Arènes de Lutèce: Jussieu, Carinal Lemoine, and Place Monge.

In 1869 Théodore Vaquer, French archaeologist and architect, rediscovered the ancient arena, which had been lost for over a thousand years. While building a tramway stop and the new Rue Monge, the construction unearthed parts of the arena walls. Restoration of the arena did not begin until author Victor Hugo founded the Société des Amis des Arènes to save further destruction. Although the park was opened in 1892, Jean-Louis Capitan directed and financed most of the restoration work, which was completed during World War I. The square adjacent to the arena bears Capitan's name.

The Roman arena sits next to the Sorbonne Université Campus Pierre et Marie Curie and less than a city block from the beautiful Jardin des Plantes. Nestled next to the campus is the Arab World Institute. Lively and inexpensive student cafes abound on Rue Mouffetard. Walk the street on market day; it's one of the best in the city.

The park at the Arènes de Lutèce

Chapter 11. Jardin des Plantes

"We will now discuss in a little more detail the struggle for existence."
Charles Darwin (1809–1882)

A large park, Jardin des Plantes offers an incredible display of flowers during the warmer months, a series of national museums dedicated to life on Earth, and a wonderful children's zoo, the Menagerie.

During the late seventeenth and early eighteenth century the Jardin des Plantes played a crucial role in the development of the science of natural history. It was at this park that much of the pioneering work was achieved in the fields of botany and zoology leading to the modern disciplines of evolutionary biology and taxonomy.

1635: Louis XIII establishes the Jardin de Roi, an herb garden for France.

In 1626 Louis XIII bought land adjacent to the Abbey of Saint-Victor with the long-term purpose of developing an herb garden for medical study. The abbey, founded in 1113, was a well-established university known throughout Europe. The theologian Peter Abélard taught here, while Saint Thomas à Becket studied at the garden prior to becoming the Archbishop of Canterbury.

Louis XIII's physician, Guy de La Brosse finished the garden in 1635 and opened the garden to the public in 1640, making it one of the first public gardens in France. Guy-Crescent Fagon, botanist and physician to Louis XIV, hired Joseph de Tournefort a brilliant botanist. Tournefort, who coined the word herbarium, furthered the concept of genus and its difference from species, and proposed the binomial system of classification. Tournefort's extensive collections from the Pyrenees, Greece, and Turkey, greatly expanded our knowledge of plant diversity. Decades later Antoine Laurent de

Jussieu, at the now renamed Jardin des Plantes, wrote the *Genera Plantarum* in 1789, which significantly improved the taxonomy of flowering plants. Seventy-six of his taxonomic families are still recognized.

Jardin des Plantes

1739–1788: Buffon, founder of modern natural history

In 1739 Georges-Louis Leclerc, count de Buffon, became director of the Jardin des Plantes. The thirty-two-year-old count was already well known for his contributions to mathematics and was a member of the French Academy of Sciences. Buffon's tenure at the Jardin des Plantes had far reaching consequences. Written from 1749 to 1788, Buffon's, *Natural History*, was one of the most widely read treatises in the world. Buffon's conclusions contributed to the sciences of biogeography, cosmology, geology, evolutionary theory, taxonomy, and population biology. Many of Buffon's ideas clashed with the theology of the clerics at the Sorbonne, which got him into trouble with the Catholic Church. At a time when most Europeans thought the Earth was just over 4,000 years old, Buffon proposed the Earth was over 75,000 years old. Buffon first suggested the idea of the "struggle for existence" in the animal world, and that life be studied within an evolutionary context. Buffon's writings were a significant influence on the works of Cuvier, the father of paleontology, and Lamark, one of the first evolutionary biologists.

Buffon's Needle
If we throw a needle, of a known length, onto a planked floor, where all the boards have an equal width, what is the probability the needle will lie across one of the seams between two boards? The Count de Buffon's mathematical solution to the problem is one of the first applications of integral calculus to a probability solution within a geometrical construct. His solution is still named Buffon's Needle.

1851: Sir Francis Head's amusing review of the Jardin des Plantes

Sir Francis Head's informative and entertaining travelogue, *A Faggot of French Sticks or Paris in 1851*, was based on his four-month stay in Paris. Head's writing style is revealed in his description of exhibited snakes in the Jardin des Plantes. Head wrote, "After passing some very large, lazy, soft, flabby boa constrictors under glass, and kept warm by blankets and hot air, in short, looking altogether very much like highly respectable aldermen after a civic feast…"

Historical snippets from the Jardin des Plantes

1792: When the Convention moved the royal zoo from Versailles to the Jardin des Plantes, one of the animals was an African lion. The zookeeper at the garden, perhaps ignorant of the diet of a lion, offered the predator a live dog for dinner. However, the lion not only refused to kill and eat the dog, but befriended the canine.

June 30, 1827: The Pasha of Egypt gives King Charles X a giraffe, the first ever seen in Paris.

In 1860 Emile Zola was often seen during the winter months warming himself on the park benches of the Jardin des Plantes. Living in absolute poverty, Zola had no heat in his room.

In 1871 during the Franco-Prussian War, when Paris was under siege, Parisians ate Castor and Pollux, the zoo's two elephants.

How to get there: Metro stations Jussieu and Gare d'Austerlitz are located next to the park. The Jardin des Plantes is situated along the Quai Saint-Bernard and bordered by Rue Buffon and Rue Cuvier. A scenic walk along the Seine through the Jardin Tino-Rossi ends at the main entrance to the park.

The Jardin des Plantes is home to the Natural History Museum of France. The Grande Galerie de l'Évolution, Galeries d'Anatomie comparée et de Paléontologie, and the Galerie de Botanique, offer spectacular displays of life on Earth. If you have children, the park offers the Galerie des Enfents and the small zoo, the Ménagerie du Jardin des Plantes. The Grande Mosquée de Paris is located along the backside of the park. As mentioned in the previous chapter the Le Jardin des Arènes de Lutèce and the Jardin des Plantes are a short distance from each other

James Bowers

Shady path through the Jardin des Plantes

Jardin Tino-Rossi

Chapter 12. Le Jardin de Cluny

"Veni, vidi, vici." (1) Julius Caesar (100–44 BCE)

View of Le Jardin de Cluny facing boulevard Saint-Germain

One can walk right by the garden of the Cluny museum and not see it. Bordering the crowded boulevard Saint-Germain, a high iron fence and dense undergrowth obscures the garden. The Hôtel de Cluny with its garden, houses the The Musée national du Moyen Âge – Thermes, established in 1843. The six *Lady and the Unicorn* tapestries highlight the museum's collections. Visitors interested in horticulture will be amply rewarded in the garden with displays reminiscent of the medieval abbeys of France.

Stand in the garden of the Hôtel de Cluny, gaze down to the busy Boulevard Saint-Germain below, and daydream back 2,000 years. In 52 BCE

Julius Caesar had defeated Vercingetorix and the combined Celtic tribes at the Battle of Alesia. All of Gaul was now a Roman province. This is the Roman city of Lutetia. Below was the river Seine, busy with commercial boat traffic. Behind you stood the city's large bath complex, what the historian Edward Gibbon called the Palace of the Baths, now the site of the Hôtel de Cluny. Further up the hill from the river, eventually to be named Sainte-Geneviève, was a temple dedicated to the goddess Diana. Beyond this temple stood a large city forum with enclosed porticos for city government and business. Further up the hill where the Luxembourg Gardens are located today, an open area existed for Rome's legionnaires to assemble and drill. The name Lutetia disappeared at the end of the fourth century when the city of the Celtic tribe Parisii became known as Paris.

The site of the Hôtel de Cluny has been occupied continuously since the birth of Christ. The baths and palace complex housed the Roman emperors Constantine, Chlorus, Julian the Apostate in the fourth century, and Clovis I in the sixth century. Becoming an abbey in 1334, Jacques d'Amboise, abbot of Cluny, completely rebuilt the complex from 1485 to 1500. The Valois kings lived in the Cluny during the Renaissance. Throughout the eighteenth century it was principally a celestial observatory. A physician owned the Cluny circa 1790 and converted the beautiful Flamboyant Chapel into a dissection room. In 1843 Alexandre du Sommerard gave the Hôtel de Cluny to France with its treasure of medieval artifacts.

November 27, 511: Savage succession in the Merovingian Dynasty

In 496 Clovis I made Paris his capital, in 508 he took up residency in the Palace of the Baths, and in 511 Clovis died as king of all the Franks founding the Merovingian line of French monarchs. They were to rule France until 754. True to the tradition of the Salian law, Clovis divided the kingdom between his four sons, Chlodomer, Childebert, Theuderic, and Clotaire. Chlodomer inheriting the Kingdom of Orléans, died in May, 524 at the Battle of Vézeronce against the Burgundians. Chlodomer's death left his kingdom without a ruler, which included the wealthy cities of Tours and Poiters.

Clotilde, wife of Clovis I, took custody of Chlodomer's three sons, Gontaire, Théobald, and Clodoald, for safekeeping. However, her other two sons, Clotaire and Childebert, wanting to divide up Chlodomer's kingdom, had another plan. They sent an ally, Arcadius, to Clotilde with the following demand. Arcadius, brandishing a pair of shears and a knife, gave Clotilde a choice for the boys' future. She could cut off the boys' hair and send them to a monastery to become monks and renounce any claims to Chlodomer's kingdom, or Clotaire and Childebert would execute the boys.

Clotilde, knowing that sending the boys off to a monastery would only produce another civil war, told Arcadius to hand over the boys to her sons. Gonaire and Théobald, seven and ten years old respectively, were stabbed and strangled to death. The assassinations ensured a stable transfer of authority. Clodoald, the third son, escaped, cut his long hair off, and joined the church eventually becoming an abbot.

Clovis's son Childebert became king of Paris in 511 at his father's death and reigned until his death in December 558. During a war with the Visigoths in 542, Childebert returned to Paris with the tunic of Saint Vincent. Childebert constructed the monastery of Sainte-Croix-et-Saint-Vincent to hold the priceless relic. The monastery later acquired the name we know today, Saint-Germain-des-Prés.

Plaque commemorating the reign of Queen Clotilde

On Christmas Day 496, Clovis I converted to Catholicism at the request of his wife Clotilde. It was a decisive juncture for Christianity in Europe. Arianism was the competing sect in the Christian faith. Arians believed that God created Christ as separate and subordinate. The First Council of Nicea in 325 deemed Arianism as heresy. Catholicism believed God the Father, Jesus, and the Holy Spirit are one being invoking the principle of consubstantiality. Clovis's influence over the region reversed the Arian dominance in the coming decades with Catholicism eradicating Arianism.

March 3, 1515: Mary Tudor marries Charles Brandon in the Hôtel de Cluny.

Mary Tudor, sister to Henry VIII, was an unhappy woman. Mary's unhappiness began on October 9, 1514, when at the age of eighteen, Mary married the sickly fifty-two-year-old Louis XII of France. The marriage sealed a treaty between England and France and gave Louis one last chance to produce the all-important male heir. For the future Francis I, the dauphin, this marriage was a surprise, and a disaster for his desire to ascend the throne of France. Francis and his domineering mother, Louise of Savoy, had spies at court watching Mary's every move. If Mary had a son, Francis would never be king. Surprisingly, Francis became quite taken with Mary, which terrified Louise. The idea of Francis possibly siring the next king of France was unthinkable. On January 1, 1515 Louis XII died, whereupon the court had Mary immediately transferred from the Hôtel de Tournelles to the Hôtel de Cluny for six weeks to make sure Mary was not pregnant.

Henry VIII's minister, Cardinal Wolsey, wrote to Mary about her future marriage plans, and horrified her with the suggestion of Charles of Flanders. No! Her brother had promised her she could select her next husband, and Mary had already fallen for the young and handsome Charles Brandon, First Duke of Suffolk. To make matters worse, the newly crowned King Francis I came to her suggesting she marry the Duke of Savoy and remain in France. Fortunately for Mary, Charles Brandon was coming to Paris to attend the coronation of Francis I, and more importantly, retrieve Mary and return to England. Prior to leaving, King Henry made Brandon promise not to wed Mary in France. On March 3, 1515 Mary Tudor married Charles Brandon in the Hôtel de Cluny, officially committing treason. King Henry softened, and permitted the marriage to stand, although Henry forced Brandon to pay a large fine to the crown. Mary lived out her life in quiet contentment in Westhorpe, Suffolk, where she died on June 25, 1533.

Francis I and his wife, Claude of France, attended the wedding of Mary and Charles. Another young woman, one of Claude's Maids of Honor, witnessed the marriage. She was to be a Queen of England, Anne Boleyn.

In 1953 Walt Disney created a romanticized version of Mary Tudor in the film, The Sword and the Rose, starring Richard Todd and Glynis Johns.

1634–1636: Superpower diplomacy: Cardinal Mazarin moves into the Hôtel de Cluny as the Papal ambassador to France during the Thirty Years War.

Politicians, lobbyists, and their schmoozing are timeless. Our story is set at the Hôtel de Cluny and its garden beginning in 1634. It reads like a play I entitle, *A Life in Three Acts.*

Act One—Getting to Know You

The Thirty Years War, begun in 1618 and lasting until 1648, pitted Protestant Germany, Sweden, and Catholic France against the Catholic Holy Roman Empire of the Hapsburgs of Germany, Austria, and Spain. The Catholic Hapsburgs wanted to extinguish the Protestant movement in northern Germany, while the Protestant states wished independence from the Catholic Church and the Hapsburgs. Catholic France, fearing encirclement by the Hapsburgs in Spain, Holland, Germany and Austria, allied with the Protestants. France kept out of the conflict through the Treaty of Bärwalde, signed in January 1631. By the treaty France funded the Swedish army with an annual stipend of 400,000 Reichstalers, to support an army of 36,000 soldiers. The treaty worked briefly without having to spill French blood.

Enter our young career-driven hero, Jules Raymond Mazarin. He made his first trip to France in 1631 as a papal legate to the court of Louis XIII and his First Minister, Cardinal Richelieu. Mazarin met with Richelieu for the first time and witnessed the construction of the Palais Cardinal, known today as the Palais-Royal. During a second trip in June 1632, Mazarin spent six weeks in Paris, again as a papal legate. Mazarin facilitated his friendship with Richelieu with paintings for the Cardinal's new palace, toilette waters, and jasmine scented gloves. Most importantly Louis XIII himself presented

Mazarin to the Queen, Anne of Austria. Mazarin impressed Anne with his manners, enthusiasm for life, and good looks. Mazarin's visits to the French court were to represent the interests of the Papacy of Pope Urban VIII. The Pope continually strove to keep a balance of power in Europe during the Thirty Years War to preserve the independence of Italy and enlarge the Papal States. Mazarin's job was to work towards that end.

Act Two—Ingratiate Yourself to Those in Power

In the summer of 1634 Urban VIII ordered Mazarin to Paris to be the new Nuncio Extraordinary or ambassador to France. In November 1634 Mazarin arrived in Paris and took up residency in the Hôtel de Cluny. Mazarin's mission was to keep France from joining Sweden and the Protestant German states in the war against the Catholic Hapsburgs. He failed.

On September 6, 1634 the combined forces of Spain and the Holy Roman Empire routed the Swedes and Protestant Germans at the Battle of Nördlingen. Months later Hapsburg armies approached the very gates of Paris. In response Louis XIII declared war on the Spanish Hapsburgs. Although France's entry into the war disappointed Urban VIII, Mazarin stayed on in Paris for another year. During this time Mazarin was seen to be under the influence of Richelieu and the French court. The Hapsburgs persuaded the Pope to recall Mazarin, and send him to Avignon to await further orders. On January 17, 1636 the Pope dismissed Mazarin following his failure in Paris. Mazarin straightaway went to work for Cardinal Richelieu and the government of France as a member of the French court. In April 1639 Mazarin became a French citizen.

Mazarin had one passion in common with the Queen of France that facilitated his rise in the French court, a love of gambling. One evening Mazarin won so often there were stacks of gold coins at his table. The winnings drew a large crowd. With Queen Anne beside him, Mazarin told the crowd the Queen's presence brought him luck. He offered her fifty thousand *écus*, a generous share of the winnings. Anne at first protested, but then accepted the winnings. Days later Mazarin learned that the King and Queen of France were most impressed with his behavior and considered him a great friend of the court.

Act Three—Timing is Everything

Setting the stage for his ultimate promotion, First Minister Richelieu sent Mazarin to Savoy to defend the regency of Christine, Duchess of Savoy, which was being contested by her brother-in-law, Thomas of Savoy. Mazarin not only solidified Christine's regency, but convinced Thomas to sign a secret treaty with France pledging mutual friendship. For this Mazarin was made a Cardinal in December 1641. Richelieu, just prior to his death in December 1642, recommended Mazarin as his replacement to Louis XIII. Six months later Louis died, whereupon Queen Anne had Mazarin take control of the French government until Louis XIV came of age. Cardinal Mazarin was First Minister of State until his death on March 9, 1661.

Statue of Adam, created around 1260 in Musée national du Moyen Âge – Thermes et hôtel de Cluny.

The museum and garden so impressed Herman Melville in 1849 that he used the Hôtel de Cluny and the Roman baths to symbolize mankind's inner spirit in the novel Moby Dick (1851). Ishmael speaks. "Winding far down from within the very heart of this spiked Hôtel de Cluny where we here stand--however grand and wonderful, now quit it; --and take your way, ye nobler, sadder souls, to those vast Roman halls of Thermes; where far beneath the fantastic towers of man's upper earth, his root of grandeur, his whole awful essence sits in bearded state; an antique buried beneath antiquities, and throned on torsoes!" (2)

Garden of the Hôtel de Cluny

From 1747 to 1784 the Hôtel de Cluny was an important astronomical observatory under the direction of Joseph-Nicolas Delisle and Charles Messier. Using a 100 mm refracting telescope, mounted on the roof of the building, Messier discovered over 110 celestial objects, designated as "Messier objects M1 to M110." Modern astronomers still utilize Messier's nomenclature.

How to get there: Use metro station Cluny-La Sorbonne. The museum and garden are situated on the south side of the Boulevard Saint-Germain between boulevard Saint-Michel and Rue Saint-Jacques. Entrance to the Hôtel de Cluny and the museum is located behind the museum on Rue du Sommerard. A short walk down boulevard Saint-Michel from the Cluny is another of our parks, the Luxembourg Garden.

The Cluny garden offers a quiet retreat for pedestrians along the busy Boulevard Saint-Germain. Like medieval gardens, the Cluny garden consists of a wooded area, an herb garden, a vegetable garden, and flowerbeds.

This is the Latin Quarter, home of the Université Sorbonne-Paris. Are you a book lover? Wander along the Rue des Écoles and boulevard Saint-Michel and visit book sellers of all types. Nestled in the center of this area is France's national mausoleum, the Panthéon, containing many of France's greatest heroes. The shops and eateries along the Boulevard Saint-Germain are limitless.

Chapter 13. Jardin du Luxembourg

"There is nothing left because if it were left it would be left over." (1)
Gertrude Stein (1874–1946)

On any weekend the Luxembourg Garden is a three-ring circus without the price of a ticket. The children's playground is a ninety-decibel chorus of munchkins doing what children do in a playground. Parents pray for exhausted offspring. The large pond in the middle of the garden hosts small-scale regattas while ducks cruise between children's sailboats. The Théâtre des Marionnettes du jardin du Luxembourg entertain children beginning each March and lasting into the fall. Small gatherings of chess players welcome spectators. I enjoy watching the action on the pétanque courts. Young couples smooch between sips of soft drinks. The Musée du Luxembourg, the city's first public museum, which opened in 1750, offers art admirers several presentations throughout the year. Many of us just come to sit and watch the show and perhaps bring a lunch. We wonder what Queen Marie de Medici, the park's creator, would have thought of this circus today.

On April 2, 1612 Marie de Medici, widow of Henry IV, Queen Regent of France, and mother of the future Louis XIII, purchased the Hôtel Luxembourg from the Duke of Luxembourg for 90,000 livres (One hundred livres were a year's salary for a physician, or the cost of a prized horse.). While living in the Louvre Palace, she enjoyed the grounds of the Duke's villa, where the Queen walked with her son Louis. Marie commissioned Italian architect Salomon de Brosse to design a new palace similar to the Pitti Palace in Florence, her childhood home. Wishing to have a park like those in Italy, Marie planted over 2,000 elm trees in the surrounding grounds and had landscape architect, Tommaso Francini, design and construct a garden behind the palace in the Italian style.

In its over four-hundred-year history the Luxembourg Palace has been home to the kings and queens of France, a prison during the Revolution, headquarters for the German Luftwaffe during World War Two, and today the home of the Senate of France. The Luxembourg Garden too, has a rich history. Napoleon and Josephine enjoyed strolls here, along with Gertrude Stein, Victor Hugo, Alexander Dumas, Ernest Hemingway, George Sand, Frederic Chopin, Isadora Duncan, and the lovers, Marius and Cosette, from Victor Hugo's *Les Misérables*.

March 18, 1662: Blaise Pascal inaugurates the first public bus line in the world.

Blaise Pascal, France's genius scientist and philosopher, initiated Paris's first public bus line, utilizing a horse-drawn carriage called a *carrosse*. The bus route ran from the Luxembourg Garden to the old Port Saint-Antoine, today the Place Bastille. The company soon closed due to high-ticket prices and a law permitting just the aristocracy to use the service. Bus service returned to Paris in the 1820s.

The Luxembourg Palace and Garden

May 21, 1717: The Duchess of Berry hosts Peter the Great in the Luxembourg Palace.

It is difficult to create a more controversial woman in French history than Marie Louise Elisabeth d'Orleans, the Duchess of Berry. Born at the Palace of Versailles and raised in the Palais-Royal, Louise Elisabeth, nicknamed Joufflotte for her chubby cheeks as a child, was the daughter of Philippe II, Duke d'Orléans. A headstrong princess, used to getting her own way, Louise married the Duke of Berry on July 6, 1710 at Versailles. It was a stormy marriage racked by scandal. After three years of marriage, the Duke took on one of Louise Elisabeth's servants as his mistress, while she in turn, began affairs with at least two lovers. Their stormy marriage embarrassed the king and court. The Duke once kicked Louise in public, while chastising her. When the Duke died of injuries sustained during a hunting accident in May 1714, the Dowager Duchess of Berry assumed ownership of the Luxembourg Palace and Garden. Initially Louise tried to close the gardens to Parisians, but there was such a public outcry from such notables as Jean-Antoine Watteau, France's premier landscape painter that she rescinded her decision.

Already known for drunkenness and a lifestyle mimicking the notorious Messalina, the merry widow hosted epic parties in the Luxembourg Palace. The most famous of all was the night of May 21, 1717 when the Duchess hosted Peter the Great, Tsar of Russia. The Duchess shocked guests that night with her risqué gown that emphasized her large bosom. The Parisian journal, *Gazette de la Régence*, reported that the Duchess was again, *puissante comme une tour*, "stout as a tower." She was pregnant.

Voltaire got himself thrown into the Bastille over the affair. He accidentally called Louise Elisabeth a whore in the presence of a police informer. Paris officials immediately incarcerated him. Voltaire inferred that the father of the child was none other than her father, the Regent. While in the Bastille, Voltaire wrote, *Oedipus*, which at that time was taken to refer to the Regent and his daughter. Premiering at the Comédie-Française in November 1718, the play was a great success, even with the Regent in attendance. Louise Elisabeth was likewise present thus completing the couple of Oedipus and Jocaste from the play!

On April 2, 1719 the Duchess delivered a stillborn girl after a life threatening four days of labor in the Luxembourg Palace. The father was probably Sicaire Nicolas d'Aydie, the Chevalier de Rion, an officer of the guards. Never recovering, she retired to the Château de la Muette and died a painful death on July 21, 1719. Louise Elisabeth was buried in the royal necropolis at the Basilica of Saint-Denis.

May 28, 1727: The Duke of Crussol kills Count Rantzau in a duel at the Luxembourg Garden.

Dueling in the seventeenth and eighteenth centuries was common amongst the French aristocracy. Beyond the dramatic nature and often fatal outcome of these contests, were the acceptable reasons for initiating a duel. This duel is a perfect example. There are other versions of this episode, but they all follow a similar plot. One night seventeen-year-old Charles-Emmanuel de Crussol, the Duke of Crussol, was attending the opera. Often the Duke brought a small box of candies having two compartments. One compartment contained delicious sweets for the ladies near him, and the second compartment contained a confection named a, *dragée*, an almond covered with sweet dough. Only the Duke had doctored the *dragées* to have a bitter taste. The Duke gave one as a prank to a Count Rantzau. The Count was greatly embarrassed in front of friends who laughed at him as he struggled with the bitter taste. The Count accosted the Duke with insults as to his character and behavior. Days later the young Duke was still furious at the Count's insults. Egged on by the Duke's mother, the Duchess d'Uzes, the Duke challenged the Count Rantzau to a duel with épées in the Luxembourg Garden. The challenge seemed foolhardy given that the Count Rantzau was a large, strong, and athletic man, and the teenaged Duke was small and hunched-backed due to a terrible wound received in an earlier combat. Nonetheless, after wounding each other slightly, the Duke finally killed the Count, all over a practical joke.

March 31, 1794: The Revolutionary Committee of Public Safety arrests Georges-Jacques Danton and Camille Desmoulins.

It was called the Reign of Terror. The Place del la Revolution, the present Place del la Concorde had the streets covered with blood from its guillotine. Adjacent neighborhoods complained of the stink. The Luxembourg Palace was now a prison. The palace garden was an industrial site full of forges for the making of breech locks and barrels for rifles. France's revolutionary Republic was fighting for its life against Europe's monarchies.

Georges-Jacques Danton and Camille Desmoulins, along with Maximilien Robespierre, were members of the most radical Montagnard faction of the Revolution, and in opposition to the Girondists, the more moderate political faction. After purging the National Convention of the Girondist faction, Robespierre continued the purges to purify the Montagnard party, which meant arresting Danton and Desmoulins and holding them in the Luxembourg Palace.

Every day Desmoulins's wife, Lucile, walked around the Palace hoping to see her husband. For the past eight years they had often walked in the garden as they lived nearby. It was in the Luxembourg Garden that sixteen-year-old Lucile Duplessis had first witnessed Desmoulins giving a speech, which led to their romance. Witnesses recalled the painful conversations between the two at the Palace after Desmoulins's incarceration. On April 5, 1794 Desmoulins and Danton, along with thirteen others, were guillotined. Desmoulins had written to Lucile that he could not conceive that men could be so vicious and unjust.

The Terror continued for the Desmoulins family. Days later Lucile was arrested for treason for trying to free her husband and was guillotined on April 13, 1794. In a letter to her mother, Lucile wrote, "A tear falls from my eyes for you. I shall go to sleep in the calm of innocence. Lucile."

On November 9, 1799 Napoleon Bonaparte overthrew the French Republic's Directory by a coup d'état electing himself First Consul for ten years. Napoleon and his bride, Joséphine de Beauharnais, moved into the Luxembourg Palace as their official residence. The couple was often seen walking in the garden.

Plaque commemorating Lucile Duplessis Desmoulins

December 7, 1815: The Chamber of Peers of France has Marshal Ney executed by firing squad in the Luxembourg Garden.

Michel Ney was one of Napoleon's greatest commanders, and a Marshal of the Empire. His career and life mirrored the turbulent and convulsive period in Europe from the beginning of the French Revolution in 1789, through the Napoleonic Wars, and ending with the Restoration in 1815. The son of a barrel-cooper, Ney studied to be a notary. Since a career as a government bureaucrat was unsuited for Ney's persona, he joined the king's army in 1787. Although Ney began as a noncommissioned officer being a commoner, he quickly distinguished himself. In May 1804 the Emperor Napoleon named Ney one of the first Marshals of the Empire with the command of a Corps in the Grande Armée. After further distinctions in Germany, Portugal, and Spain, Marshal Ney led a corps in the invasion of Russia in 1812. During the disaster of Napoleon's retreat from Russia, Marshal Ney played a crucial role as a rear-guard commander, and was known as the last Frenchman in Russia. On April 4, 1814 Ney spoke on behalf of the French army and confronted Napoleon demanding his abdication. Ney's actions earned the respect of Louis XVIII, who knighted Ney and made him a peer of France.

When Napoleon escaped from Elba and began the Hundred Days War, Ney committed treason and joined Napoleon in March 1815. Although he fought with legendary bravery at Waterloo, the monarchy had Ney arrested and tried for treason. On the morning of December 7, 1815 at the back of the Luxembourg Garden, a firing squad executed Michel Ney. He refused to wear a blindfold and demanded to command his own execution. Marshal Ney's name is one of the six hundred sixty heroes of France inscribed on the walls of the Arc d'Triomphe.

April 5, 1818: Karl Drais introduces the world's first patented balance bicycle in the Luxembourg Garden.

Baron de Drais, born in Karlsruhe, Germany, invented the first patented balance bicycle named the *Laufmaschine*, "running machine." First tested in Mannheim in June 1817, the Baron introduced the bicycle in the Luxembourg Garden in 1818. The French called it a *velocipede*, while in England and Germany, it was named a *draisienne* after the inventor's name. Constructed totally of wood the bicycle immediately became popular with Parisians. Impractical to ride on anything but a smooth surface, the bicycles were custom made based on the rider's size. By the 1860s French companies had added handle bars, crank pedals, and adjustable seats to a metal frame.

An early *draisienne*, the world's first patented bicycle circa 1818.

March 1832: Cholera reaches Paris.

It is easy to forget how more than a century ago, diseases such as cholera, diphtheria, and tuberculosis, were everyday killers. In 1832 an inadequate supply of clean drinking water and the absence of an effective sewage disposal system created a cholera epidemic in Paris. Baron Haussmann's modernized sewers were still decades away.

The dead were brought to the city morgue beside the Hôtel de Ville for identification and removal. Amandine-Aurore-Lucie Dupin, pen name George Sand, and one of France's greatest novelists, was living on Île de la Cité during the cholera outbreak. Instead of walking to the city morgue to find out if any friends had died, Sand and her associates gathered each evening in the Luxembourg Garden to see who was still alive. Weeks were to pass before the routine ended.

"Masterpieces are only lucky attempts." (2) George Sand (1804–1876)

March–July 1844: The Three Musketeers

First serialized in the Paris newspaper *Le Siècle* between March and July 1844, Alexander Dumas's *The Three Musketeers*, was set in the neighborhoods around the Luxembourg Garden in 1626. The story in Paris begins, "Thus d'Artagnan entered Paris on foot, carrying his little packet under his arm, and walked about till he found an apartment to be let on terms suited to the scantiness of his means. This chamber was a sort of garret, situated in the Rue des Fossoyeurs, near the Luxembourg." Athos too, lived in the neighborhood. Dumas wrote, "Athos dwelt in the Rue Ferou, within two steps of the Luxembourg." Aramis lived on the Rue Vaugiraud overlooking the garden.

The inspiration for the story of *The Three Musketeers* originated from Dumas' research into the life of Louis XIV, and stumbling upon a novel entitled, *Memoirs of Sir d'Artagnan, Lieutenant Captain of the first company of the King's Musketeers*, by Gatien de Courtilz de Sandras, published in Cologne in 1700. In the preface of *The Three Musketeers*, Dumas gave full credit to de Sandras for the story.

"Tous pour un, un pour tous, c'est notre devise." (3) Alexander Dumas (1802–1870)

A path through the Luxembourg Garden

1900: American dancer Isadora Duncan dances in the Luxembourg Garden.

Dancing with the Augustin Daly dance company in London since 1898, Isadora Duncan was unhappy with the conformities of the company and moved to Paris in 1900 with her mother, Mary, a brother Raymond, and a sister Elisabeth. Every morning Isadora and her siblings practiced their dancing in the Luxembourg Garden, which was near their studio on the Rue de Villiers. Tragically on September 14, 1927 in Nice, Isadora's long scarf got caught in the rear wheel of her car and strangled her to death.

1903: Gertrude Stein takes an apartment next to the Luxembourg Garden and establishes the Stein Salon.

In 1903 after a year in London, Gertrude Stein and her older brother Leo moved into an apartment at 27 Rue de Fleurus a block west of the Luxembourg Garden. Gertrude's Saturday evening salons were in part, to define modern art and literature of the twentieth century. Along with Alice Toklas, who became Gertrude's lifelong partner in 1907, the writers, Ezra Pound, Sinclair Lewis, F. Scott Fitzgerald, Guillaume Apollinaire, Thornton Wilder, and Ernest Hemingway were regular attendees. Here the Steins befriended Pablo Picasso, Henri Matisse, and Georges Braque, and began gathering their famous collection of Impressionist paintings.

> "You look ridiculous if you dance
> You look ridiculous if you don't dance
> So you might as well dance." (4)
> Gertrude Stein (1874–1946)

The park became part of Gertrude's life. When she visited Picasso's studio, she always cut through the park to catch the Odéon omnibus to Montmartre. Gertrude took walks in the Garden with her poodle Basket. When Hemingway became close friends with Miss Stein, he walked in the park with Gertrude, his first wife Hadley, and their infant son Jack, nicknamed Bumby. During these years at the Luxembourg, Stein wrote, *Q.E.D.* (Quod Erat Demonstrandum), *Fernhurst*, *Three Lives*, and *The Making of Americans*.

Many Americans like myself, learned some of their French by watching the PBS television series, French in Action. Professor Pierre Capretz of Yale University developed the French language course, which became popular with an almost cult-like following. The immersion course featured the story of a young American man visiting Paris named Robert, played by Charles Mayer, and a young French woman, named Mireille, played by Valérie Allain. Several episodes that featured the younger sister to Mireille, Marie-Laure, played by Virginie Contesse, were filmed at the Luxembourg Garden pond where Marie-Laure sailed her model boat. Whenever I visit the Luxembourg Garden,

I am always reminded of those episodes, and enjoy watching the children sail their boats.

The Grand Bassin in the Luxembourg Garden

American author and lecturer Helen Davenport Gibbons lived all through World War One in Paris on Rue Servandoni only a few hundred meters from the Luxembourg Palace and Garden. In April 1918 Helen recorded that one of the huge shells from the Paris Gun landed one afternoon and blew away a corner of the Grand Bassin behind the Palace where her children sometimes played. Helen did not mention whether anyone was injured.

1936–1937: The Luxembourg Garden apiary

In 1936 and 1937 Richard Le Gallienne wrote respectfully two charming travel books on Paris titled, *From a Paris Garret* and *From a Paris Scrapbook*. Le Gallienne's apartment (a seven-story walk up), bordered the Luxembourg Garden, one of his favorite locations. One afternoon Richard was grocery shopping at one of the large stores on the boulevard Montparnasse. While musing over a delicious looking plum cake, he suddenly noticed a swarm of honeybees around him and the cake. One of the store's salesmen pointed out a small plate of brown sugar, used as a decoy, covered with bees. The salesman declared that all the bees come from the apiary in the Luxembourg Garden, and that they range far and wide over the city.

Later that afternoon, Le Gallienne met the bees again at a small *épicerie* across the street from Les Deux Magots, the famous *brassière* on the boulevard Saint-Germain. The owner informed Le Gallienne that the Luxembourg bees raided over most of the Left Bank of Paris. A society of apiculture ran the small bee village in the park, which was open to visitors on certain days for lessons in bee keeping. Le Gallienne stated that the honey was quite delicious.

Founded in 1856 by Henry Hamet, the Beekeeping School of the Luxembourg Garden offers annual classes and certificates for the keeping of honeybees. The parent organization, the Central Society of Apiculture, maintains similar apiaries in the Parc Georges Brassens and the Parc Saint-Cloud.

1940–1944: German occupation of the Luxembourg Palace and Garden

From June 14, 1940 to August 25, 1944 Nazi Germany occupied Paris. During the occupation the German Luftwaffe used the Luxembourg Palace and its garden complex as its headquarters in France. Hermann Göring, the head of the Luftwaffe, had a sumptuous office in the Palace throughout the war.

Days leading up to the liberation of Paris saw the oddities and tragedies of war. On August 20, 1944 Clara de Chambrun, an American living across the street from the garden, watched a young woman riding a bicycle, fire several pistol shots at a passing German armored vehicle. The German vehicle returned with automatic fire shattering every single window in Clara's building.

Beekeeping School of the Luxembourg Garden

On August 23, as the Nazi's hold over Paris weakened, French resistance units of the Forces Françaises de l'Intérieur (FFI) began to challenge the Germans. In one instance several FFI were captured at the Luxembourg Garden. The Germans forced them to dig a large pit, where they were immediately shot and buried. The bodies were discovered after the liberation of Paris.

The Luxembourg Garden was one of the strong defensive points for the Germans in the security of Paris. On the day of the liberation several hundred soldiers from the SS Standartenführder Division and the 6th Fallschirm Panzer Jäger Division dug foxholes around the grounds. In the garden panzers fired across the park towards the Rue Vaugirard. Starting near the Place de l'Odéon, armed units from the 501st Tank Regiment of Free French Army LeClerc Division attacked the German defenders. The Luxembourg Garden was one of the last positions held by the Germans prior to their surrender.

When King Robert the Pious died in 1031, his place of residence, the Château Vauvert, was abandoned. Located where the Jardin Robert-Cavelier-de-La-Salle and the Jardin Marco Polo are situated today, the deserted palace quickly became a haunt of thieves and the homeless. Superstitious local residents began believing that the devil haunted the ruins. Hence the French proverb, aller au diable Vauvert, go to the Vauvert Devil, was born. In English we just say, Go to the Devil!

How to get there: Metro stations RER Luxembourg, Odéon, Notre-Dame-des-Champs, and RER Port Royal are all within a few blocks of the palace and garden. The Boulevard Saint-Michel, Rue de Vaugirard, Rue Guynemer, Rue Auguste-Comte, and Rue de Médicis, border the garden. I have grouped the Jardin Robert-Cavelier-de-La-Salle, and the Jardin Marco Polo with the Luxembourg Garden because all three a form contiguous green space.

If you're looking for quiet moment in Paris, the western part of the Luxembourg Garden along the Rue Guynemer has a serene ambience—a good place to sit, read, or picnic.

Pleasures are never-ending in the sixth arrondissement. Consider dinner at Le Procope, founded in 1686, and dine where Voltaire, Franklin, and Jefferson drank a new and exotic liquid called coffee. Browse along the Quai des Grand Augustins and shop for second-hand books at the bouquinist stalls. Have a quiet moment in a pew of the Église de Saint Germain des Prés open since the sixth century. Be a rubbernecking tourist ogling store fronts along the boulevard Saint-Germain.

View through the Jardin Robert-Cavelier-de-la-Salle towards the Luxembourg Garden

The Fountain of the Observatory, also named the la Fontaine des Quatre-Parties-du-Monde, created by Jean-Baptiste Carpeaux, Pierre Legrain, and Emmanuel Fremiet in 1874.

Chapter 14. L'Esplanade des Invalides

"There are only two forces that unite men — fear and interest." (1)
Napoleon Bonaparte (1769–1821)

On November 24, 1670 King Louis XIV ordered the construction of Les Invalides, a home for aging and disabled soldiers. Completed in 1676 this complex featured fifteen courtyards and a chapel, the Église Saint-Louis des Invalides, which was finished in 1679. The Sun King added a second chapel, the Église du Dôme, as a private royal chapel. The remains of Napoleon Bonaparte reside in the Église du Dôme.

Situated along the Seine, the large open esplanade in front of the Invalides has existed for centuries. In 1544 Parisians used this large field for mass burials due to the plague. Catholics buried Protestant dead in the esplanade after the Saint Bartholomew's Day massacre in 1572. During the First World War this grassy field played a crucial role in the defense of Paris.

September 6, 1914: Paris taxicabs save the city during the First Battle of the Marne.

On June 28, 1914 Yugoslav separatist Gavrilo Princip assassinated the Archduke Franz Ferdinand of Austria and his wife Sophie in Sarajevo, Bosnia and Herzegovina. The Hapsburg Austro-Hungarian Empire declared war on Serbia, which triggered a complicated series of responses according to treaties amongst the Triple Entente of France, the British Empire, and the Russian Empire, against the Central Powers of Germany and Austria-Hungary. Following the Schlieffen Plan Germany first invaded neutral Belgium and Luxembourg before attacking France in August.

By September 1, 1914 units of the German army were less than ten miles from the gates of Paris along the Marne River. On September 2, the French government evacuated Paris and moved to Bordeaux. Although he had retired in the spring of 1914, General Joseph Gallieni, was named Governor of Paris, and assigned to defend the city. Gallieni immediately prepared the city to defend itself, stockpiling supplies for the city, clearing woods and bridges for artillery fire, and laying plans for the demolition of the Eiffel Tower and major bridges on the Seine. He informed the government in Bordeaux that he was also making plans to evacuate Paris.

Hôtel des Invalides and esplanade

On September 6 on the esplanade of the Invalides, Gallieni commandeered 1,500 Paris taxicabs to ferry over 6,000 troops to the front just east of Paris. As the First Battle of the Marne developed, the French viewed the taxicab army of Gallieni as the saviors of Paris. Each taxi could carry five soldiers, four in the back seat and one with the driver in the front. All of the taxicabs were demobilized on the next day, and were paid for their time.

George Perris, a British journalist attached to the British headquarters in Paris, was an eyewitness to events. He wrote.

"I went out into the deserted countryside toward the front, passing marching columns, motor-wagons, dispatch-riders, here a flock of sheep with uniformed shepherds, there a woodland bivouac, and in the evening returned to Gagny. More regiments had arrived; the town was boiling from end to end. In the main street, a battalion was already marching out to extend Vautier's left, a thin file of country folk watching them, waving handkerchiefs, the girls running beside the ranks to give some handsome lad a flower. Up the side roads, other columns waited their turn, standing at ease, or sitting on the edge of the pavement; a few men lay asleep, curled up against the houses. But the most curious thing was a long queue of Parisian taxi-cabs, a thousand or more of them, stretching through by-roads out of sight. The watchful and energetic Gallieni had discovered, at the cost of us boulevardiers, a new means of rushing reinforcements to the point where they were direly needed. – The 7th Division had detrained in Paris during the afternoon of September 7. It was to be sent to Maunoury's extreme left, near Betz, forty miles away. Everything might now depend upon speed. Only about a half of the infantry could be carried quickly by train. Clergerie thought the remaining six thousand men might be got out by means of taxicabs. The Military Government of Paris already had one hundred of the "red boxes" at its disposal; five hundred more were requisitioned within an hour, and at 6 p.m. they were lined up, to our astonishment, beside the Gagny railhead. Each cab was to carry five men, and to do the journey twice, by separate outward and return routes. Measures were taken in case of accident, but none occurred. This first considerable experiment in motor transport of men was a complete success; and at dawn the 7th Division was in its place on the battlefield." (2)

The First Battle of the Marne proved to be one on the most significant of World War I. The Allied victory for France and Great Britain ended Germany's hope for a quick success promised by the Schlieffen Plan.

Germany's nightmare of a protracted two-front war with Russia to the east and the Allies to the west proved fatal.

> *When large numbers of American soldiers were stationed in Paris during World War I, the Americans built a baseball diamond on the esplanade.*

How to get there: The metro and RER stations named Invalides are located along the Seine and the Quai d'Orsay.

The esplanade of the Invalides is the front lawn of two historical attractions in Paris, the Museum of the Army and Napoleon Bonaparte's tomb set within the Église du Dôme. A treasure in the museum is a 1905 Renault taxi that took part in the Battle of the Marne by ferrying troops to the front on the night of September 6, 1914. Adjacent to the Invalides along the boulevard des Invalides is the Rodin Museum containing the best works of the French sculptor Auguste Rodin. Enjoy a coffee or tea surrounded by Rodin's sculptures in the garden behind the museum.

The seventh arrondissement is home to one of the most visited attractions on Earth. Begun in 1887 and completed in 1889 for that year's world's fair, Gustave Eiffel's tower is the very symbol of Paris. Drawing a world-wide audience is the nearby Musée d'Orsay, holding the world's largest collection of Impressionist art.

Chapter 15. Parc du Champ-de-Mars

"Mr. Watson. Come here. I want to see you."(1)
Alexander Graham Bell (1847–1922)

The Parc du Champ-de-Mars is always busy with tourists visiting the Eiffel Tower. Tour buses fill the street along the front edge of the park beginning each morning and remain well into the evening. Like most of the large parks in Paris the Champs-de-Mars is filled on the weekends with local residents enjoying the large lawns and playground areas for the children.

Positioned between the École Militaire to the southeast and the Eiffel Tower to the northwest, the Parc du Champ de Mars was named after ancient Rome's Campus Martius, "Mars Field", where Rome's legionnaires assembled and drilled. Mars was the Roman god of war.

The park began as the Plain of Grenelle, where neighborhood farmers grew vegetables and flowers for the city markets. After the École Militaire was built in 1752, the grass field in front of the military school, hosted French troops for marching exercises. Such a large green space within the city was conducive to a series of spectacular events covering several facets of French history for over two centuries.

August 27, 1783: Jacques Charles launches the first hydrogen balloon in the Parc du Champ-de-Mars.

Having studied the works of Robert Boyle and Henry Cavendish, Jacques Charles believed that hydrogen would make an excellent gas to provide lift for a lighter-than-air balloon. Charles first designed a small spherical balloon and collaborated with the Robert brothers, Anne-Jean Robert and Nicolas-

Louis Robert, for its construction. Brilliant engineers, the Robert brothers invented a light airtight balloon made from silk and sealed by a rubber coating. On the day before the flight the team started filling the balloon with hydrogen in the Robert brothers' workshop located at the Place des Victoires. Approximately a quarter of a ton of sulfuric acid was poured over a half ton of scrap iron, which liberated hot hydrogen gas. The hydrogen was next passed through lead pipes into the balloon. The filling of the balloon attracted a large crowd necessitating an open area. Charles and the Robert brothers moved the balloon to the Champ-de-Mars.

Parc du Champ-de-Mars

On August 27, 1783 the little balloon was released and after a northward flight lasting over half an hour the balloon landed northeast of Paris, near the village of Gonesse. The citizens of Gonesse, having never seen such a thing, immediately attacked the balloon with pitchforks as if it were an alien creature from the heavens. Fellow scientist, Benjamin Franklin, witnessed the flight.

Later in the year Jacques Charles and Nicolas Robert made the first manned hydrogen balloon flight from the Jardin des Tuileries on December 1, 1783. This later flight covered over 35 kilometers and lasted over two hours. Over 400,000 French watched the event including Benjamin Franklin.

Those of us who have worked with sulfuric acid in the laboratory, know that sulphuric acid is extremely dangerous, and even the slightest inhalation or contact with the skin is instantly painful and damaging. When reading how Charles generated the hydrogen gas, my imagination shudders at how dangerous this operation must have been, and wonders if anyone was injured in the process.

In 53 BCE Julius Caesar set up a temporary camp in the village of Lutetia Parisiorum to deal with the rebel Senones and Carnutes Celtic tribes. After Caesar left the region the local tribe, the Parisii, joined the Celtic rebellion. Caesar's lieutenant, Titus Labienus, returned and defeated the Parisii commander Camolugenus on the plain of Grenelle where the Champs de Mars and the École Militare are situated today.

July 14, 1790: The first Bastille Day is celebrated on the Champ-de-Mars.

France held its breath and hoped that the worst of the Revolution's civil chaos was finished. The newly created constitutional monarchy celebrated with the first Bastille Day. Celebrating the one-year anniversary of the storming of the Bastille and the new constitution, the holiday was originally named the *fête de la Fédération* in honor of the voluntary soldiers, named *fédérés*, in the National Guard. Louis XVI and his centuries old Bourbon regime momentarily accepted their new status in the republic. The National

Assembly decided to hold a celebration of unity on the Champ-de-Mars, because it offered a large space at the edge of Paris. Volunteers assisted in the preparations with "wheelbarrow days" to construct two gigantic earthen embankments for the spectators, a triumphal arch at one end of the grounds, and a large tent to house the King and court. In the center of the field, workers built a large altar for the members of the National Assembly and the King to hold mass and swear allegiance to the forthcoming constitution. Charles Maurice de Talleyrand-Périgord, then Bishop of Autun, gave the mass. Louis spoke, "I, King of the French, swear to use the power given to me by the constitutional act of the State, to maintain the Constitution as decreed by the National Assembly and accepted by myself." The Marquis de Lafayette, representing the National Assembly, swore a similar oath to the constitution. After the celebration a large meal was prepared for approximately 20,000 citizens at the nearby Chateau de la Muette.

This was the first time the United States of America flew the Stars and Strips flag on foreign soil. Heroes of the American Revolution, Thomas Paine and John Paul Jones, represented the United States. The celebration was a wonderful moment for the French Revolution prior to the onrushing future tragedies. The Bastille Day celebrated today originated in a law that was made official on July 6, 1880 during the Third Republic.

July 17, 1791: The Champ-de-Mars Massacre

On July 15, 1791 the National Assembly declared that King Louis XVI would remain the King of France ruling over a constitutional monarchy. The Assembly furthermore searched for an excuse to suppress the radical Republicans of Paris who wanted to destroy the Bourbon government. The Republicans were outraged. Jacques Pierre Brissot, editor for the journal *Le Patriote français*, proposed a petition to nullify the Assemblies' declaration, and asked citizens to gather on the Champ-de-Mars to sign it. Two days later over fifty thousand French Republicans rallied at the Champ-de-Mars. Lafayette, commander of the National Guard, dispersed the gathering, but during the confrontation the Guard fired on the crowd killing more than fifteen citizens and wounding tens of others. The Champ-de-Mars Massacre, as it became known, briefly suppressed Republican ambitions, but they exploded again in the near future. The killings ruined the reputation of Lafayette, and the Paris citizenry never trusted the general again. The bloody incident had wider repercussions increasing the gulf between the middle-class bourgeoisie and the commoner. The Republicans never forgave the Bourbon regime.

June 8, 1794: Robespierre's Festival of the Supreme Being at the Champ-de-Mars

In order to understand this unusual public celebration, which brought tens of thousands of French to the Champ-de-Mars, one must revisit a fundamental cause of the French Revolution. Although the socio-politico-economic causes were complex, one reason was obvious in 1789, the privileged status of the Roman Catholic Church. Like the Bourbon nobility, the Church paid no taxes and accumulated immense wealth over the centuries. By 1789 the Catholic Church was a major landowner in France along with the nobility. The line between church and state was moreover blurred with Cardinals Richelieu and Mazarin managing the state. Church leaders lived in extreme luxury, while most of the French lived in severe poverty. These social and economic disparities nourished a deep resentment in much of France especially with the desperately poor.

During the First Republic, beginning in 1792, the government made a concerted effort to suppress the Church in France. A Cult of Reason at first became popular, as a civic religion emphasizing truth, liberty, and virtue. Unbelieving in supernatural beings the cult's god was the People of France based on the Enlightenment's tenants of reason. The quasi-religious movement incensed antirevolutionary forces and revolutionaries loyal to the Church. Radical Jacobins such as Maximillien Robespierre were infuriated and struck back against the cult. In 1794, as leader of the Committee of Public Safety, Robespierre sought to replace the Cult of Reason with a form of Deism, named the Cult of the Supreme Being. Worshiping god in the traditional sense, the cult believed in the immortality of the soul. However, god in this form of Deism was not of a revealed religion—not discovered by natural reason alone. God did not intervene in the world in a supernatural sense. Robespierre's god was revealed according to the natural laws of the universe. The cult existed during the brief Reign of Terror under the leadership of Robespierre and reached its peak during the celebration on June 8, 1794. Orchestrated by the painter Jacques-Louis David, the festival drew

James Bowers

tens of thousands of French, who came to worship and celebrate the new state religion dedicated to public virtue on the grounds of the Champs-de-Mars.

After Robespierre's fall from power and subsequent execution on July 28, 1794, the cult quickly disappeared. Napoleon Bonaparte sealed the cult's fate and others like it, when Bonaparte passed the Law of Cults banning them on April 8, 1802. Napoleon went on to welcome the return of the Catholic Church to help consolidate his power and regime.

> *"Citizens, did you want a revolution without a revolution?" (2)*
> *Maximilien de Robespierre (1758–1794)*

1867–1937: The Parc du Champ-de-Mars hosts five world's fairs.

World's fairs became popular during the nineteenth century. The Industrial Revolution was the principal impetus; fairs let countries and industries market their products and services to a global audience. In 1844, Paris hosted its first world's fair, called the French Industrial Exposition, which was housed in a temporary building on the Champs-Élysées. Not to be outdone, Great Britain followed up with the famous London Great Exhibition of 1851, known as the Crystal Palace Fair due to the immense glass exhibition hall. France answered with the International Exhibition of 1855, again located on the Champs-Élysées.

The Champ-de-Mars was chosen for all future fairs as the park gave Paris a much larger space and a perfect location on the Seine for transportation. Five international fairs were held on the park grounds in 1867, 1878, 1889, 1900, and 1937. They offered an endless variety of entertainment on a larger-than-life scale.

International Exposition of 1867

In 1864 Emperor Napoleon III decided to hold another world's fair in Paris to aggrandize his regime and showcase Baron Haussmann's new Paris. Opening on April 1 and continuing to November 3, the International

Exposition of 1867 featured exhibits from over forty countries. The main exhibition hall was enormous, even by today's standards. The length exceeded 1,600 feet and the width over 120 feet.

Japan's exhibit of woodcuts at the Exposition had a profound influence on European and American art for the remainder of the century. Contemporary artists, such as Vincent Van Gogh, James McNeill Whistler, and Claude Monet, incorporated Japanese themes and styles into subsequent works.

> *One of the celebrities attending the fair was French author Jules Verne. Impressed and inspired by the exhibitions on the possibilities of electricity, Verne wrote his classic, Twenty Thousand Leagues Under the Sea (1870), which featured Verne's electrically powered submarine, the Nautilus.*

1878: Paris World's Fair of 1878

The Paris World's Fair of 1878 was the largest world's fair to date with over thirteen million visitors. On the hill of Chaillot across the Seine from the Champ-de-Mars, fair organizers built the Moorish looking Trocadéro Palace, a concert hall named in honor of the French victory at the 1823 Battle of Trocadéro, Spain. Three popular attractions were American: Alexander Graham Bell's telephone, Thomas Edison's phonograph, and Frédéric Bartoli's Statue of Liberty.

In 1865 the American Civil War ended. Édouard René de Laboulaye, law professor, politician, historian, and poet, was a staunch supporter of the Union. A fierce abolitionist and chairman of the French Anti-Slavery Society of France, Laboulaye came upon the idea of building a statue for America to celebrate the end of slavery in the United States and the continued friendship between the two countries. He turned to his good friend, the sculptor Frédéric Bartholdi, for help in making his idea a reality. Bartholdi designed a neoclassical figure of the Roman goddess, Libertas, representing liberty. The goddess held a torch of freedom and a, *tabula ansata*, a tablet evoking the law, which was inscribed with the date of the Declaration of Independence, July 4, 1776. The statue's official name is, "Liberty Enlightening the World" (*La Liberté éclairant le monde*). In order to construct the 150-foot statue, Bartoli contracted Gustave Eiffel to engineer and construct the statue, which had an internal iron frame and a copper cladding skin. On June 30, 1878 the completed head of the statue was debuted on the fairgrounds in front of the Trocadéro Palace. The goddess's face was rumored to resemble Bartoli's mother. Other pieces were displayed on the Champ-de-Mars. After years of fund-raising efforts to complete the statue, the Statue of Liberty was finally shipped to the United States and dedicated at Liberty Island, New York City, on October 28, 1886.

The global fair provided a forum for two important meetings. The Congress for the Protection of Literary Property, led by the French novelist Victor Hugo, was able to draft a series of proposals, which became the world's first international copyright laws. Concurrently, the International Congress for the Amelioration of the Condition of Blind People brought to the world the first use of the Braille tactile writing system.

Napoleon Bonaparte wanted a system of communication for his soldiers without requiring light or sound during the night. He gave the project to Captain Charles Barbier, who developed a system of night writing for the French army. In 1821 the French Royal Academy of Sciences asked Barbier to present the system to the Royal Institute for Blind Youth, the first school in France for blind children. In the audience was Louis Braille, blinded by an accident at the age of three. Barbier's night writing system used raised embossed dots for the reader to feel, but the system was slow and complicated. Braille simplified and streamlined Barbier's system into the Braille system used worldwide today.

1889: The Universal Exposition of 1889 featuring the Eiffel Tower

The Universal Exposition of 1889 celebrated the one-hundred-year anniversary of the storming of the Bastille, which marked the beginning of the French Revolution. Gustav Eiffel's tower and the Buffalo Bill Wild West show starring Annie Oakley were the stars of the fair for the approximately twenty-eight million attendees.

Replica of the Statue of Liberty on the Allée des Cygnes, Paris

The Latting Observatory, a 315-foot tower at the 1853 Exhibition of the Industry of All Nations in New York City, inspired French engineer Gustav Eiffel to build a similar tower for the 1889 world's fair in Paris. Eiffel instructed two civil engineers, Swiss born Maurice Koechlin and Frenchman Émile Nouguier to design and engineer the tower. Both worked for Eiffel's firm, Compagnie des Établissements Eiffel. The construction began on January 28, 1887 and finished on March 31, 1889 with the exception of the complicated elevator systems. A huge sensation, over 1.8 million tourists visited the Eiffel Tower during the exposition. Gas lanterns illuminated the tower at night with three searchlights— red, white, and blue— throwing pencil beams over the Paris night sky. The Eiffel Tower proved to be indispensable during World War I as the tower was ideal for military radio transmitting and listening.

William Frederick Cody, known to the world as Buffalo Bill, was born on February 26, 1846 in the little town of Le Claire, Iowa. Cody lived an extraordinary life. He was a Pony Express rider at the age of fourteen, fought in the American Civil War for the Union at the age of seventeen, and won the United States Medal of Honor in 1872 for his bravery in the Indian Wars.

Cody acquired the name, Buffalo Bill, when he signed a contract with the Kansas Pacific Railroad to supply buffalo meat to the crews. Cody became famous throughout the west as a hunter, scout, and war hero. His life changed when Edward Judson, penname Ned Buntline, published the dime novel, *Buffalo Bill, the King of Border Men* in the *New York Weekly* beginning on December 23, 1869. Ever the publicist and showman, Buntline went on to adapt his novel as a successful theater production. Meeting in December 1872, Cody joined Buntline's theater company to act in The Scouts of the Prairie, one of the first wild west shows. Cody toured with the Buntline shows for a decade, then in 1883, Cody started his own traveling show entitled, Buffalo Bill's Wild West.

Two years later famous sharpshooter, Phoebe Ann, "Annie" Oakley, joined Cody's show and starred at the 1889 Exposition. The daily show opened with a parade of stars on horseback featuring cowboys and Indians. Shows featured mock stagecoach robberies, sharp shooting by Annie Oakley, Indian attacks on settlers of the old west, and portrayals of the Pony Express postal system. Cody included a reenactment of the Battle of the Little Bighorn, where Plains Indians overwhelmed General Custer's army. After the Exposition of 1889 Cody's show toured throughout Europe for another year with great success.

1900: Fifty million visitors attend the Universal Exposition of 1900 and the Games of the II Olympiad on the Champ-de-Mars.

The 1900 International Exposition celebrated the beginning of the twentieth century. Opening on April 15 and closing on November 12, the fair hosted the first Olympic games to be held outside of Greece. Unlike previous fairs, the 1900 Exposition spread out over the city beyond the park grounds of the Champ-de-Mars and the area of the Trocadéro Palace.

Three iconic edifices were built to accommodate the fair, the Pont Alexander III, the Grand Palais, and the Petit Palais. The Alexander III Bridge, built in the Beaux-Arts style and named after the Russian Tsar, connected the temporary exhibition halls located on the esplanade of the Invalides with the Grand Palais. Having an exterior façade in the Neo-Baroque-like architecture, the Grand Palais was home to an automobile show, horse shows, and a sculpture garden. The Petit Palais was designed in the Art Nouveau style with elements of the Neo-Baroque. The Petit Palais featured the history of art from primitive beginnings to the present including a special history of French art from 1800 to 1900. Today the Petit Palais is home to the City of Paris Museum of Fine Arts.

Two inventions, ubiquitous to modern life, were featured, the diesel engine, and talking motion pictures. Rudolf Diesel first ran his diesel engine on August 10, 1893 in Augsburg, Germany. Patented in the same year, Diesel successfully leased production rights throughout Europe for a wide variety of purposes. At the 1900 Exposition Diesel demonstrated his engine running on peanut oil. Within a decade Diesel's engines were in service on a global scale.

As early as 1888 Edward Muybridge and Thomas Edison collaborated on the Kinetoscope to produce a moving picture with sound. However, the device only allowed a single viewer at a time. Inventors Henri Lioret and Maurice Gratioulet of France, improved upon the cylinder-based recording technology to produce the Phono-Cinéma-Théâtre, which projected the image on a screen with synchronized sound. Spectators at the Exposition were treated to the first projected talking motion pictures. The sound quality was poor and the synchronization of image and sound was inconsistent. High quality talking motion pictures did not appear until 1927.

In addition to the 1900 Universal Exposition, the Champ-de-Mars was the administrative center for the 1900 Games of the Second Olympiad. The first modern games held in Athens in 1896 were a great success and held promise for the next games to be held in Paris at the 1900 Exposition. Unfortunately for the Olympic movement the games were commercialized to complement the Exposition and took on carnival-like themes. Historically, these games are now considered a bad example of the Olympic spirit. In addition to being the first Olympic games to be held outside of Greece, it was the first Olympics where women competed.

Quite different from today's games, sports such as croquet, automobile and motorcycle racing, firefighting, tug-of-war, and ballooning were included. In one of the shooting events live pigeons were used as targets. Recognized as the poorest Olympics ever held, the International Olympic Committee did not sanction the games.

The Exposition of 1900 was a financial disaster. The cost of organizing, creating, and maintaining the facilities overwhelmed revenues. Consequently, the periodic hosting of international expositions in Paris as an economic stimulus, ended. Another thirty-seven years passed before Paris hosted another world's fair.

1937: International Exposition of 1937—Hitler versus Stalin

World's fairs have always been a showcase for competing nations to propagandize economic and political agendas. The International Exposition of 1937 was no exception. Europe was struggling with the economic depression, which furthered the ambitions of fascist Germany. The 1937 world's fair in Paris, from May 25 to November 25, was the perfect venue to contrast the radical differences between Adolf Hitler's Nazi Germany and Joseph Stalin's Communist Russia. The two contrasting pavilions dominated the fair facing each other in defiant poses. The Soviet pavilion featured a large statue entitled, *Worker and Kolkhoz Woman*, by Vera Mukhina portraying male and female workers carrying the Communist hammer and sickle. The German pavilion was a massive austere monolithic structure, crowned by the Nazi eagle and swastika. German architect Albert Speer (1905–1981) wanted a design to symbolize defiance to the Communist manifesto.

Like the 1900 world's fair, the 1937 Exposition left permanent buildings in Paris. The Palais de Chaillot houses the Museum of Man (Musée de l'Homme) and the Palais de Tokyo is now the Museum of Modern Art. The Spanish pavilion, sponsored by the leftist Republican government, featured Pablo Picasso's *Guernica* dramatizing the indiscriminate German and Italian bombings of the little village of Guernica. During the fair the Eiffel Tower transmitted the first experimental television signals in France.

The stainless-steel statue Worker and Kolkhoz Woman, (Rabochiy i Kolkhoznitsa) by Vera Mukhina has had a fascinating life. Classical statues such as the Victory of Samothrace and the Harmodius and Aristogeiton, inspired sculptor Vera Mukhina to create the monumental piece in the socialist realist style. After the fair ended, the statue was returned to Moscow, and today is a focal point in the All-Russia Exhibition Center in Moscow. A replica of the statue was featured at the 2014 Sochi Winter Olympic Games.

August 25, 1944: The French tricolor flies over the Champ-de-Mars.

Lucien Sarniguet was a Captain of the Paris fire department posted near the Dupleix metro station in the seventh arrondissement. On June 14, 1940, when the German army captured Paris, Captain Sarniguet was forced to remove the French tricolor on top of the Eiffel Tower and raise the Nazi swastika. He swore that he would return the French flag atop the tower. Four years later in the weeks prior to the liberation of Paris, wives of the Dupliex fire station took six bed sheets, dyed two red and two blue, to create the tricolor flag in anticipation of the liberation. On August 25, 1944 Captain Sarniguet and four other volunteers traversed the Champ-de-Mars field to the Eiffel Tower, and climbed the 1750 steps to return the French tricolor atop the tower, while German troops were still fighting in the park below.

Wall for Peace by Clara Halter (1942–2017) in the Parc du Champ-de-Mars

How to get there: The Trocadéro Gardens, Eiffel Tower, and Park Champ-de-Mars are all situated together spanning the Seine in the seventh and sixteenth arrondissements. The best metro station to visit the complex is Trocadéro, located in front of the Trocadéro Gardens. Station École-Militaire is located on the backside of the Champ-de-Mars park near the Rue Cler neighborhood. If you are staying in the central part of the city in the first through sixth arrondissements near the Seine, the Bateaux Bus boat taxi stops at the base of the Eiffel Tower.

The puppet theater, Les Marionnettes du Champ de Mars, located in the center of the park, features over 300 different puppets on a Napoleon III-Empire Period stage.
Visitors can occasionally hear the hooting of tawny owls in the Champ-de-Mars.

Chapter 16. Jardins des Champs-Élysées and Promenade du Cours-la-Reine

"La vie est la farce à mener par tous." (1) Arthur Rimbaud (1854–1891)

I discovered the Jardins des Champs-Elysées and the nearby Promenade du Cours-la-Reine when looking for the stamp market featured in Stanley Donen's movie, the thriller *Charade*. Positioned along the avenue des Champs-Elysées its walkways are continually busy with tourists. In quieter moments, the gardens host neighborhood workers at midday as they eat takeout lunches on the park benches. Urban growth during the reign of Louis XIV led to the park's creation.

In 1667 Louis XIV ordered architect, André Le Nôtre to expand and improve the Tuileries Gardens. Le Nôtre extended the gardens in a straight line several hundred meters from the Place del la Concorde along the new avenue. It was named Grande allée du Roule, which changed to the Avenue des Tuileries, and a third time to Avenue de la Grille-Royale, until Avenue des Champs-Elysées was finally decided upon in 1789 during the Revolution. Champs-Elysées means Elysian Fields, which were the fabled resting places for Greek heroes. The new park accompanying the avenue eventually was named Jardins des Champs-Elysées. In 1840 Jean-Charles Alphand patterned the most recent version from English designs. The gardens uniqueness to the history of Paris lies in its residing alongside the most famous street in Paris, the Champs-Elysées. For centuries Parisians have used the gardens to witness and participate in some of the most significant moments in French history

Marie de Medici, daughter of Francesco I de Medici, married Henry IV in 1600. Henry was deep in debt and Marie brought a handsome dowry. She grew up in the Pitti Palace in Florence, where a common pastime was coach riding in the parks along the River Arno. Living in the Louvre Palace as Queen of France, Marie planted four rows of elm trees creating three pathways for carriage rides. It was named the Cours-La-Reine. During her reign, the Cours la Reine became a fashionable meeting place for nobility as they enjoyed the coach rides along the Seine. Built in 1616 the Cours La Reine is one the oldest green spaces in Paris.

Cours-La-Reine

October 5, 1789: The Women's March on Versailles

It was eighty-one days since the fall of the Bastille, and Paris was hungry. Bread, the staple of the French diet, was costly and scarce. A loaf of bread was worth near a year's wages for many of the poor. September grain shipments to Paris were far below what was needed. Parisians blamed Louis XVI and his regime for having deregulated the grain markets in 1774, which resulted in shortages every year. Famine was ever present. Many in Paris believed that the monarchy was planning to starve the population.

In October 1789, deliberations at the National Assembly frightened the King, and to secure his safety and the government's, Louis ordered the Flanders Regiment of the Army to occupy Versailles. This act did not provoke the populace, but on the night of October 2, a large banquet was held at Versailles to welcome the troops. The royal family was in full attendance at this sumptuous party with an abundance of bread. Revolutionary publications such as Éllsée Loustalot's *Révolutions de Paris*, reported the event and emphasized the soldiers' disrespect for the tricolored cockade, while feasting at the expense of the poor. Parisians were enraged.

On the morning of October 5, a *poissarde*, a fishwife or market woman, near the Church of Sainte-Marguerite, grabbed a drum, began beating it and marched down the street demanding bread for Parisians. By the time the woman reached the Hôtel de Ville a crowd of women had joined her. The women attacked the weakly guarded city hall and made off with hundreds of muskets and a few cannons. Leaving the Hôtel de Ville, this growing assemblage marched in the rain through the city, the Tuileries Gardens, the Gardens of the Champs Elysées, and the relatively new Avenue des Champs-Elysées. Over the next six hours this ragtag horde slogged its way in the mud to the palace at Versailles. Heightening this dangerous situation, the National Guard, 15,000 strong, decided to join the *poissardes* in protest. The Marquis de Lafayette, commander of the Guard, was forced to allow their participation for fear of his life. The *poissardes* had already reached Versailles by the time the Guard left Paris.

Wet, hungry, and exhausted, the *poissardes* horde was stopped at the iron gates of the Versailles Palace. Besides massing at the gates, large numbers of the *poissardes*, who had not joined in the march to Versailles, invaded the National Assembly back in Paris to protest the food shortages. Louis agreed to the Declaration of the Rights of Man that afternoon, due in part to the *poissardes*. By the evening thousands of National Guardsmen finally arrived at Versailles. On the morning of October 6, 1789, the King's government and the National Assembly, defended by the Flanders Regiment, the Versailles National Guard, and the Hundred Swiss, found itself surrounded by a large armed group of revolutionaries. Lafayette was in an impossible position to keep both sides calm in this explosive situation.

Having found an unlocked gate into the royal apartments, revolutionaries raced towards Marie-Antoinette's rooms. Two guards tried to stop them. One was immediately slain and his head put on a pike. Hearing the scuffle, the Queen ran barefoot down the halls with her children to Louis's private bedroom and after frantically banging on the door they were finally united with the King. The Queen and family were saved when a few of the National Guard with the *poissardes* stood by to protect them.

Moments later a haggard Lafayette arrived to save the royal family and in doing so, saved the monarchy. Lafayette walked Louis onto the balcony over the Cour de Marbre where Louis agreed to accompany the National Guard back to Paris and place his family in the Guard's safety. Lafayette further defused the situation by pinning the tricolor cockcade onto the hat of a sergeant of the king's guard resulting in a roar of approval from the crowd. Completing this face-saving political gesture, Lafayette brought out a reluctant and severely frightened Marie-Antoinette onto the balcony. In what could have been a political disaster, Lafayette kissed the hand of the Queen and raised it to the crowd. The *poissardes* and guardsmen cheered wildly with shouts of "Vive la reine." Later King Louis XVI and his court left for Paris in coaches amidst a walking crowd of thousands. Wagons filled with flour accompanied the family as a gesture to help Paris. The future of the regime was now in the hands of the Assembly and the Guard.

The Declaration of the Rights of Man and of the Citizen was a civil rights statement drafted by the National Constituent Assembly in August 1789. Patterned after the 1776 United States Declaration of Independence, the document was included in the constitutions of the Fourth French Republic and the Fifth French Republic. Derived from the political themes of the

Enlightenment, the Declaration held that civil liberties were a right of all mankind.

November 11, 1918: Armistice signed ending World War One

At the eleventh hour and the eleventh day of November 1918 church bells rang over Paris celebrating the allied victory ending the First World War. Huge crowds of Parisians flooded the Champs Elysées gardens in celebration. Similar celebrations were later held in the gardens for United States President Woodrow Wilson's visit for the peace talks at Versailles on December 16, 1918. Marshall Ferdinand Foch, Supreme Allied Commander, celebrated the Allied victory on Bastille Day July 14, 1919 with an even larger parade along the gardens.

Remember Audrey Hepburn and Cary Grant running through the stamp market in the 1963 thriller movie Charade? Named the Carré Marigny, this Paris landmark was established in 1864, and still thrives today on the Rue de Marigny along the Jardins des Champs-Elysées.

How to get there: The metro stations Concorde, Franklin D. Roosevelt, and Champs-Élysées Clemenceau are located at the Jardins des Champs-Élysées and near the Promenade du Cours-la-Reine. Visitors staying in the first through seventh arrondissements are within walking distance to the park.

Two annual events take place on the Avenue des Champs-Élysées and its Jardins des Champs-Élysées, the Tour de France bicycle race and the Bastille Day parade. Began in 1903 the Tour de France has ended in Paris at the Arc de Triumphe since 1975. Race day is on a Sunday, during the third week of July. Celebrating the capture of the Bastille prison on July 14, 1789, the Bastille Day parade was made official on June 28, 1880. It is one of the oldest parades in the world.

Jardins des Champs-Élysées

Having lived for a month a few blocks from the Avenue Champs-Élysées, I can attest that the eighth arrondissement is a patchwork of contrasts. The area is more cosmopolitan than ever before, epitomizing the nature of international wealth. Contrast the shopping for the super-rich along the Avenue Montaigne and Rue Saint-Honoré to the busy middle- and upper-class residential streets scattered throughout the district.

Chapter 17. Parc Monceau

The word *monceau* means "a pile of, a heap of."

The Boulevard Périphérique is a veritable racetrack ringing Paris. A small-scale equivalent exists within the Parc Monceau. Every weekday during the lunch hour the walking path surrounding the Parc Monceau is filled with a similar traffic flowing by at varying speeds. Joggers have replaced the high-speed automobiles, lane-hopping motorcycles, and lumbering semi-trucks. Adding to this midday madness are packs of children on recess from the adjoining neighborhood schools who surge up and down the arterial pathways running through the park. Park benches are likewise filled with the lunch crowd from nearby businesses. The whole is an entertaining rush hour exemplifying the energy of a great metropolis. Equally, the Parc Monceau can provide a serene experience with its ancient trees, placid views around its pond, and remnants of the original English folly. We can thank the Duke of Chartres for the Parc Monceau.

1779: A theme park for Paris or Philip's Folly

On June 6, 1769 Louis Philippe d'Orléans, the Duke of Chartres, married Louise de Bourbon, daughter of his cousin, the Duke of Penthièvre, the richest man in France. The next day Louis Philippe purchased a small tract of land without any specific purpose on the edge of Paris, called Montchaut.

Nine years pass by and the Duke decided, for reasons unknown today, to build a public park in Paris. The Duke was a close friend of the Prince of Wales (the future George IV), and loved everything English. He commissioned Louis Carrogis Carmontelle, a writer, architect, and painter, to create an English garden or folly. The word folly is an architectural term, meaning a structure designed principally for ornamentation or decor without a practical use other than entertainment. Eighteenth-century follies were gardens composed of several themes representing different eras and cultures.

Remnants from the original Monceau Folly

When the park was completed in 1779, the attractions featured a grape vineyard housing a minaret, a Tar Tar tent, a Swiss dairy farm, a small pond named La Naumachie surrounded by a Roman colonnade, a Roman temple to Mars, the ruins of a Gothic castle, a Chinese village with a pagoda-roofed temple, and a small pyramid with an accompanying obelisk. Servants dressed in clothing from the Orient along with their camels mingled with the guests. The folly was short lived. In 1781 Scottish landscape gardener Thomas Blaikie extensively remodeled the garden.

1784: *Le mur murant Paris rend Paris murmurant ("The wall walling Paris keeps Paris murmuring", [anonymous])*

Did government outsourcing cause the French Revolution? Not entirely, but the Bourbon regime's outsourcing of tax collecting to a private tax-farming corporation created a corrupt system, which the French deeply resented. It was called, the *Ferme Générale*, literally translated as the "general farm."

In 1784, the situation worsened when the Ferme Générale started to construct a wall circling the city of Paris. Charles Alexandre de Calonne, the Controller-General of Finances, brought in the famed architect Claude-Nicolas Ledoux to design the wall. The purpose of the wall was to ensure that no one entered or left the city without paying their taxes. The Wall of the Farmers-General was positioned alongside the Park Monceau with one of the main gates built at the edge of the park. When construction was completed in 1791, the wall was twenty-four kilometers long with gates placed every six kilometers. One of the main tax collection gates was the Pavilion de Chartres named after the park founder, the Duke of Chartres. While the ground floor was used for business, the upper level was a private apartment reserved for the Duke. Louis Petit de Bachaumont, a famous gossip of the day, called the Wall, "a monument to enslavement and despotism."

> *Louis-Sébastien Mercier described the Ferme Générale in the Tableau de Paris (1788), as "the bastions of taxation metamorphosed into columned palaces." (1)*

Today the Pavilion de Chartres, now renamed the Rotunda, serves as the main entrance to the Park Monceau (see photo p. 158). The witticism below summed up French feelings towards the Wall on the eve of the Revolution.

Pour augmenter son numéraire (To increase its cash)
Et raccourcir notre horizon (And to shorten our horizon),
La Ferme a jugé nécessaire (The Farm judged it necessary)
De mettre Paris en prison (To put Paris in prison)
Anonymous.

James Bowers

July 14, 1789: Cannon fire from the Bastille

On the night of July 14, 1789, when Parisians were storming the Bastille, Louis Philippe, the Duke of Chartres, and the Marquis de Lafayette were enjoying a pleasant evening with their friend, Englishwoman Madame Elliott. She wrote in her diary for the evening that they heard cannon fire in the city whereupon the men left immediately. The cannon fire signaled the storming of the Bastille and the beginning of the end for Louis Philippe.

Walkway at Park Monceau
where the Wall of the Farmers-General once stood

A man of the Enlightenment, Louis Philippe was a Jacobian during the Revolution. Abandoning the Estates General the Duke joined the National Assembly. Famous for his hatred of Marie-Antoinette, Phillipe adopted the name of Philippe Égalité in 1792. During the Reign of Terror, when all the Bourbons in France were arrested, he was sent to trial and guillotined on November 6, 1793.

The state nationalized the Park Monceau on his death, but the land was returned to the Orleans family during the Restoration of Louis XVIII. In 1860 after the city of Paris purchased the land, Baron Haussmann had the engineer-architect Adolphe Alphand remodel the park into its present configuration. The current Parc Monceau opened in 1861.

Walking paths in the Park Monceau

October 22, 1797: André-Jacques Garnerin makes the first free-fall parachute descent into the Parc Monceau.

André-Jacques Garnerin's development of a frame-free silk parachute had been progressing for several years with the help of his brother, Jean-Baptiste-Olivier Garnerin. On October 22, 1797 Garnerin made the world's first parachute descent into the Parc Monceau.

Giant sycamore tree in Park Monceau

He arrived at a design that preceded today's modern parachute. The cloth part was circular-shaped. When collapsed a hollow pipe ran up through the parachute and held the assembly to a balloon above until release. Unlike a harness used today, a small wicker basket held the parachutist Garnerin. During this first descent the basket weaved about in a significant fashion, but Garnerin landed unharmed from a height of 3000 feet.

Watching in the large crowd was Jeanne Geneviève Labrosse who was soon to marry Garnerin. On October 12, 1799, from a height of 2700 feet, she became the first woman to make a parachute descent.

During the Peace of Amiens of the Napoleonic Wars, Garnerin and his wife made demonstration flights over London in a hydrogen balloon, culminating in a parachute descent into Grosvenor Square on September 21, 1802. Tragically, while working on a large balloon in a barn, a large beam collapsed killing Garnerin on August 18, 1823.

Garnerin's young niece, Elisa Garnerin, continued the family legacy. She first flew in a balloon at the age of 15 and went on to become a female daredevil throughout Europe. From 1815 to 1836, Elisa made thirty-nine descents in Russia, Germany, Spain, and Italy using the name, Prima Aeroporista (First Parachutist).

Plaque in Park Monceau commemorating Garnerin's parachute jump

James Bowers

May 21–28, 1871: The Bloody Week (La Semaine Sanglante)

Paris parks have been the scene of numerous war atrocities through the centuries. In the spring of 1871 the national government of France, based in Versailles, was faced with recapturing Paris in the aftermath of the Franco-Prussian War. The Paris Commune, a socialist leaning political faction, opposed the government and held Paris from March 18 until May 28, 1871. Park Monceau was one of several areas used by the national government of Adolphe Theirs to execute Communard partisans by firing squad. Soldiers examined everyone. If they had gunpowder on their hands from firing a rifle, they were immediately tried on the spot and shot. The exact number of Communards shot in Park Monceau is unknown. Larger scale executions ensued at the Luxembourg Gardens and Père-Lachaise cemetery. The Commune dead exceeded six thousand people with some estimates reaching twenty thousand. Government losses were approximately eight hundred fifty dead and over six thousand wounded. Historians named it The Bloody Week.

How to get there: Use metro station Monceau. Situated in the eighth arrondissement Parc Monceau lies adjacent to the busy Boulevard de Courcelles. If you are near the Arc du Triumphe and Avenue des Champs Élysées, walk along Avenue Hoche, which leads directly into the center of Parc Monceau.

Parc Monceau is different from many French city parks, in that it follows the English style of landscape architecture, featuring winding walkways and plantings suggesting idealized pastoral scenes. The columns in the park around the small pond were taken from the tombs of the Valois kings erected by Catherine de Medici at Saint-Denis.

La Naumachie basin in Park Monceau

Park Monceau possesses some of the most spectacular sycamore trees in France. One was planted in 1853, a second tree reaches a height of thirty meters, and a third one exceeds seven meters in circumference.

The Musée Cernuschi, adjacent to the park, is dedicated to Asian art featuring collections from China, Japan, and Korea.

Chapter 18. Bois de Vincennes

"O, who hath done this deed?"
Othello William Shakespeare (1564–1616)

The Bois de Vincennes, the largest park in Paris, has a zoo, a hippodrome, the Parc Floral botanical garden, and the best-preserved castle keep in Europe. This medieval fortress served as one of France's most notorious prisons. When autumn colors peak, the park offers colorful and relaxing walks. The Vincennes forest has ancient beginnings.

During the Roman era, two large forests surrounded Paris. To the east was Vilcena, where the name Vincennes originates, and to the west was Rouvray, which centuries later acquired the name Bois de Boulogne. In the middle of the twelfth century, Louis VII built a hunting lodge in the Vilcena forest, where the Bois de Vincennes and the Château de Vincennes stand today. Philippe-Auguste built a castle on top of the lodge, and in 1336 Philip VI constructed the now imposing fortress donjon or castle keep. Louis XIV expanded the château, and Louis XV opened the château grounds to the public in 1730. The park we enjoy today was created during the reign of Napoleon III and opened in 1860. His Prefect of the Seine, Baron George-Eugène Haussmann and Jean-Charles Alphand, expanded the lands around the park and lavished the grounds with amenities similar to the Bois de Boulogne. While the park was being created, architect and medieval restorer Eugène Emmanuel Viollet-le-Duc renovated the château's chapel and the castle donjon.

August 31, 1422: Henry V, King of England, dies at the Château de Vincennes.

In the last disastrous decades of the Hundred Years War the English House of Plantagenet and the French House of Valois remained in a death struggle for the throne of France. Henry V, King of England, renewed the war in 1415, and after his celebrated and surprising victory at the Battle of Agincourt, Henry became regent and heir to the French throne under the Treaty of Troyes in 1420. As part of the treaty Henry married Catherine of Valois, daughter of the French king, Charles VI. However, the war continued with a French victory at the Battle of Baugé. This forced Henry to remain in France and lead the English army.

Henry laid siege to the fortress at Meaux on October 6, 1421, which lasted into the summer of 1422. Smallpox and dysentery claimed a significant portion of Henry's army. By August Henry himself had contracted dysentery and had to be taken back to Paris. Henry chose the fortress at the Bois de Vincennes for recovery, but died suddenly on August 31, 1422. Fortunately for the Plantagenet dynasty, Henry's wife Catherine, had given birth to a son two months prior to Henry's death.

His son, Henry VI, lived an extraordinary life. As one of the chief players in the War of the Roses Henry VI became King of England and of France, fought insanity on several occasions, and had a strong and politically astute wife in Margaret of Anjou. He lost the throne in 1461, regained it in 1470, lost it again in 1471, and finally died in the Tower of London later in the year, perhaps on orders by his successor King Edward IV. Both Henry V and Henry VI were later immortalized in William Shakespeare's plays, *Henry V*, *Henry VI: Part 1*, *Henry VI: Part 2*, and *Henry VI: Part 3*.

Amongst the chaos and accepted atrocities of the era, Henry V and Henry VI contributed to the long-term cultural achievements of England. After the Norman conquest Norman French became the language of the English court. Henry V returned English as the official language last used by the Anglo-Saxon kings more than three centuries earlier. Henry VI found time between his stints of madness and running for his life to found King's

James Bowers

College, Cambridge, All Souls College, Oxford, and Eton College.

Autumn in the Bois de Vincennes

Château de Vincennes

1677–1682: The Affair of the Poisons

After the sensational trial and execution of the Marquise de Brinvilliers in 1676 for poisoning her father and two brothers, a scandalous series of murders again shocked Paris and darkened the reign of Louis XIV. The subject of several historical books and numerous academic journal articles, these murders are known today as The Affair of the Poisons. The plots read like an Agatha Christie novel with Perry Mason defending—all directed by Alfred Hitchcock.

Our drama ensued at two locations, the Paris Arsenal and the fortress at the Bois de Vincennes. As the drama unfolded Louis XIV's secret police required an undisclosed location for a tribunal hidden from Parisians. Louis's police selected the Royal Chamber of the Arsenal. Because the courtroom was lit with torches, the Chamber acquired the nickname *Le Chambre Ardente* (The Burning Chamber). The police also needed a jail to detain and interrogate prisoners. The dungeons at the Château de Vincennes, hidden from public view on the grounds of the Bois des Vincennes, were perfect.

On September 21, 1677, a year after the execution of the Marquise de Brinvilliers. An anonymous letter left in the Jesuit confessional box at a church near the Bastille, warned of a conspiracy to poison Louis XIV and his heir, the Dauphin. The king immediately ordered the head of the Paris police, Gabriel de la Reynie, to round up all alchemists and persons known for their knowledge of poisons.

Reynies first arrested Louis de Vanens, who claimed he had created gold using alchemy. The mistress of Vanens's valet, testified Vanens and his valet were both professional poisoners. Her testimony linked both of them to a Magdelaine de La Grange, a well-known fortuneteller and poisoner, recently charged with fraud and the murder of a wealthy banker. The court condemned Vanens to a life sentence in prison, where he died in 1691.

Madame La Grange was held for two years without ever revealing any information. However, after a brief trial La Grange was hanged on February 8, 1679. After the arrests and the testimonies of all involved Reynie's superior, the Marquis de Louvois, the Minister of War, believed Reynie had stumbled upon a secret group of professional assassins. The Marquis ordered Reynie to intensify his investigations.

Reynie's undercover informers were successful. Marie Vigoreaux had given a party where the fortune teller, Marie Bosse, nicknamed La Bosse, bragged about successfully selling poisons to women of high rank. After gathering more evidence, Reynie arrested Vigoureaux, La Bosse, La Bosse's daughter, and her two sons on January 4, 1679. Madame Vigoreaux died under torture later in the year. After her trial La Bosse was burned alive at the stake at the Place de Grève in front of the Hôtel de Ville on May 8, 1679. The testimonies of Vigoreaux and La Bosse implicated other ladies of standing furthering the investigations.

Minister Louvois now initiated the infamous tribunal at the Arsenal. The hearings opened with the trial of Marguerite Leferon. who had poisoned her husband, a prominent Parisian judge. Catherine Monvoisin, a suspected poisoner known as La Voison, told the police at Vincennes she had sold poison to Leferon. As a member of the bourgeoisie, the convicted Leferon was given a light sentence—banishment from Paris and a 1,500-livre fine.

Further interrogations at Vincennes led to the arrest of the Marquise de Poulaillon. The marquise was a young wife with a husband much older than herself. She had approached Vigoreaux and La Bosse for help. She was told how to poison with arsenic using a gradual technique to avoid suspicion. Monsieur de Poulaillon discovered the plot and had his wife held in a convent until the Paris city court charged her. Reynie's tribunal heard of the charges and went ahead and arrested the marquise. Interrogated on June 5, 1679, her testimony resulted in banishment from Paris, despite the Solicitor-General of the tribunal having demanded the death penalty.

Gossip reached new heights when Reynie and his now labeled, "Chamber of Poisons", arrested a Madame de Dreux, a prominent lady of Parisian society. La Bosse had implicated Madame de Dreux of trying to poison both her husband and any female who showed interest in her lover, the Marquis de Richelieu. The tribunal issued a legal warning in 1680 and released Madame de Dreux after a year in custody.

The testimonies of La Bossie and La Voison were then taken directly to the king. On December 27, 1679, Louis XIV ordered the court to aggressively pursue the poisoners' clients, regardless of rank, sex, or position. On January 23, 1680, Reynie's tribunal delivered arrest papers for the Duke of Luxembourg, the Vicomtesse de Polignac, and what was most scandalous, for Olympia Mancini, the Countess de Soissons, the Lady-in-Waiting to Maria Theresa, Queen of France. Although the tribunal kept the arrest warrants secret, word of them leaked out and created a national scandal.

François de Montmorency-Bouteville, Duke of Luxembourg, was the Captain of the King's Bodyguards and a Marshal of France. Without any real evidence the Duke was released and exonerated of all charges. The Duke went on to become one of France's greatest generals.

The Vicomtesse de Polignac sought potions from La Voison to make the king desire her, and poisons to kill the king's mistress, Louise de La Vallière. When Madame de Polignac learned of her coming arrest, she fled. The Vicomtesse was tried in absentia and sentenced to exile for life in Puy-de-Dôme, Languedoc.

The king offered the Countess de Soissons a choice, go immediately to the Bastille for trial or leave France. The Countess left for Flanders. She was charged with threatening to kill the king and his mistress, Madame de La Vallière. The Countess died in Brussels in 1708.

La Voison was subjected to the Question of the Boot. This torture, carried out at the Château de Vincennes, began by blocking a victim's legs between wooden boards. Iron bars were progressively driven in between the leg and the surrounding boards, slowly crushing the leg. La Voison denied all charges. She was burned at the stake on February 22, 1680. The Marquise de Sévigné, who followed these events, witnessed La Voison's execution. She wrote to her daughter how La Voison frantically fought her executioners when she was taken from the cart to the scaffold. In a morbid comment Madame de Sevigné complained that she and her neighborhood residents were subjected to breathing the ashes of the poisoner!

The Affair of the Poisons had one more shocking revelation—the testimony of the La Voison's daughter, Marie Montvoisin. She admitted after days of intense interrogation, to knowing the Marquise de Montespan, the mistress of Louis XIV. La Voison's accomplice, Adam Lesage, had several years earlier testified that Montvoison had held Black Masses for Madame de Montespan to bewitch the king and replace Madame de La Vallière as the king's mistress. However, the Marquise at that time was a new and an unimportant arrival to court. Lesage's testimony was ignored.

In August 1680, Montvoisin, told Reynie and Louvois that Black Masses involving satanism and witchcraft were held for Madame de Montespan. Although detailed records of her testimony have disappeared, Reynie's personal notes from the testimony revealed Reynie himself believed Black Masses were performed. In October Louis, fearing Madame de Montespan might be implicated in the Affair, ordered a cessation of the trials. Reynie agreed to continue the interrogations of Montvoisin, Lesage, and their accomplices on a secret and personal basis at the fortress of Vincennes. Months passed, while Reynie recorded testimonies. It was the king's decision to press charges against his mistress Montespan. In May 1681, Louis ordered the Arsenal trials to begin again in secret, but with one new condition. Certain testimonies were to be forever withheld for purposes of state.

All testimony regarding Madame de Montespan never reached the tribunal. As far as the king was concerned the issue was over, and ordered the tribunal to cease inquiries. The Chamber of the Arsenal closed in July 1682. No further actions took place and findings of the tribunal were never released.

Montvoison and Lesage were never officially sentenced, but were sent to die in the king's dungeons. All the state records from the Affair of the Poisons are now held in the Arsenal Library.

And what of the fate of Madame de Montespan? Louis had difficulty ending his relationship with her, given the length of their affair, seven children, and continued close friendship. By 1686 Madame de Maintenon became his mistress. Also, Louis's wife, Queen Marie Thérèsa, had died, obviating Montespan's position in court as Superintendent of the Queen's Household. By 1691 Montespan was living at the Convent of Saint Joseph and estranged from Louis. In 1700 Montespan bought the Château d'Oiron in the provence of Poitou, and lived there until her death on May 27, 1707.

Besides everyday avarice, this is a tale about superstition. In seventeenth-century France, life was perceived through a veil of the supernatural. Witchcraft, sorcery, aphrodisiacs, and fortune telling were all accepted features of French society. The beginnings of the Enlightenment were becoming apparent, when in 1672, Louis XIV and the Parliament of Paris issued edicts erasing the prosecution for witchcraft and sorcery from the legal code. The fortunetellers and poisoners in the Affair of the Poisons were charged as criminals for murder, fraud, and theft. Because of the Affair of the Poisons, Louis ordered Reynie to publish an ordinance controlling the manufacture, distribution, sale, and use of poisons on August 30, 1682. This ordinance formed the basis of the modern legal code in France governing hazardous chemicals.

July 23, 1749: French philosopher, Denis Diderot, is imprisoned in the Château de Vincennes.

Having been put on notice by the monarchy and the Catholic Church for heresy in his recent novels, philosopher and encyclopedist, Denis Diderot subsequently published anonymously, *Letter on the Blind for the Use of Those Who Can See*. This lengthy essay featured a blind English mathematician proposing many radical ideas, several heretical to Christian dogma. Most radical was the concept that man evolved without the supernatural intervention of a god, pointing the way to the evolutionary biology of Charles Darwin and Alfred Wallace. Church and state immediately knew who the author was, and on July 24, 1749 the governor of the Prison of Vincennes had his police arrest and jail Diderot. At first Diderot was held under solitary confinement under harsh conditions, but Voltaire, an admirer of Diderot's writings and with influence at court, stepped in and had his treatment greatly improved. After three months in custody, Diderot signed a restraining order prohibiting him from publishing works criticizing the state and church. Diderot was freed on November 3, 1749 whereupon he started to write the monumental treatise the *Encyclopédie, ou dictionnaire raisonné des sciences, des arts et des métiers*. Completed in 1772, Diderot had written the world's first encyclopedia. Although Diderot was famous during his lifetime, fame did not bring fortune. In order to raise money for his daughter's dowry, Diderot was forced to sell his private library to no less than Catherine the Great, Empress of Russia. Catherine allowed Diderot to keep his library until his death.

"Let us strangle the last king with the guts of the last priest." (3)
Denis Diderot (1713–1784)

1777–1784: *The Marquis de Sade is jailed in the Château de Vincennes.*

How does anyone begin to discuss anything about the Marquis de Sade? Since his death in 1814, he is virtually a household name anywhere in the world. An adjective in several languages is derived from his family name—sadistic. Here is the story of the Marquis de Sade as it relates to the Bois de Vincennes and the history of Paris.

Donatien Alphonse François, the Marquis de Sade was born to an old aristocratic family from Provence on June 2, 1740. Raised largely by household servants, he quickly gained a reputation as a stubborn wild youth. True to his noble rank, Sade joined the king's armies at the age of fifteen. A brave and valued soldier, the Marquis attained the rank of colonel during the Seven Years War. In 1763 the Marquis married Renée-Pélagie de Montreuil, who came from a wealthy business family. The union produced a daughter and two sons. An affair shocking even to the conventions of the French aristocracy overtook these inauspicious beginnings.

On the night of Wednesday October 18, 1763, the Marquis went to a Madame du Rameau on Rue Montmartre in Paris to procure the prostitute, Jeanne Testard. The next morning Rameau and Testard went to the office of Lieutenant General of Police Antoine de Sartine to complain of Sade's behavior the night before. In her deposition Testard claimed the Marquis had made her trample on the crucifix and watch the Marquis masturbate on a statue of Christ. Ten days later Sartine sent Inspector Marais, head of the vice squad to arrest the Marquis. Sade was immediately taken to the Château de Vincennes. Being a noble, the Marquis was released on probation on November 13, 1763 into the care of his wife's family. Paris police were to keep watch over the Marquis for the rest of his life.

Five years later, on Easter Sunday, April 3, 1768, the Marquis procured street beggar Rose Keller and took her to a rented house in Arcueil, near Paris. The Marquis tied Keller down on a bed, and repeatedly whipped her on three or four occasions. No sex was performed. He also forced Keller to whip him on repeated occasions. Afterwards, the Marquis left her locked in the room. Keller escaped in the evening and went to the police in Arcueil. Keller brought charges against the Marquis, but dropped them after the Marquis's mother-in-law, Madame de Montreuil, bribed her with a handsome sum of 2,400 livres. The Marquis's family had once again saved Sade from a trial and incarceration.

Four years later on June 27, 1772 the Marquis was in Marseilles to hire a troupe of actors to assist with theatrical productions in Provence. The Marquis hired four prostitutes for the day. After several hours of sodomy and whippings involving all participants, including his valet, the Marquis paid the ladies before they left. Unknown to the prostitutes, the Marquis had given the ladies treated anise candies thought to be an aphrodisiac. The next morning two of the ladies were seriously ill and believed the Marquis had poisoned them. They went to the police.

On July 4 the police arrived at the Marquis's family estate in La Coste to arrest Sade on charges of poisoning the prostitutes and sodomy, in France a capital crime. The Marquis fled before they could arrest him. Juicy news of the episode traveled fast, and in Paris, Bachaumont's popular tabloid *Mémoires secrets*, reported the Marquis was again fleeing the law for alleged deranged atrocities against prostitutes. Still on the run in September 1772, the French Parliament declared the Marquis and his valet guilty and sentenced to death. The Marquis de Sade was to be beheaded, and his valet, a commoner, hung and then strangled. Incredibly, the Marquis hid for the next five years.

On February 8, 1777 the Marquis entered Paris where Inspector Marais arrested the Marquis and immediately returned him to the prison at the Bois de Vincennes. Mother-in-law Madame de Montreuil obtained a *lettre de cachet* from King Louis XVI to keep the Marquis at Vincennes for the rest of his life. He remained at Vincennes until February 29, 1784. He became Monsieur No. 6 as his old cell No. 11 was occupied.

In near solitary confinement, the Marquis turned to writing. From 1780 to 1782 the Marquis wrote several plays, a series of letters published posthumously, and the philosophical essay, *Dialogue between a Priest and a Dying Man*.

Because the prison at Vincennes held only a handful of people and needed repairs, the government decided to close the prison and transfer the remaining prisoners, including the Marquis, to the Bastille in February 1784. Five years were to pass before a chance for freedom surfaced. During his period in the Bastille Sade wrote, *Les 120 Journées de Sodome* (120 Days of Sodomy), which was not published until 1904. Sade described the work as the most impure tale that has ever been told since the world began.

The French Revolution was a savior for the Marquis de Sade. By 1790 the National Assembly abolished the *lettre de cachet*, which was the legal instrument for incarcerating the Marquis. Sade walked out of prison a free man, but it was not to last. By 1803 Sade was imprisoned for life in the asylum at Charenton due to the language in the novels *Justine* and *Juliette*. He died on December 2, 1814 probably due to complications from pneumonia. The Marquis was buried in the asylum's cemetery with an unmarked stone. At the time of his death the sixty-four-year-old Marquis was having a sexual relationship with fourteen-year-old Madeleine LeClerc, the daughter of an asylum worker.

October 15, 1917: A French firing squad executes Mata Hari, the alleged spy for Germany, in the Bois de Vincennes.

At daybreak Father Arbaux and two accompanying nuns awakened Marguerite Zelle in the Saint-Lazare prison, while her attorney Édouard Clunet and Captain Bouchardon of the French Army looked on. The guards remarked she had slept well. Marguerite now knew President Poincaré had denied her stay of execution. A small motorcade whisked Marguerite to the old army barracks on the grounds of the Bois de Vincennes.

The Temple of Love on Lac Daumesnil in the Bois de Vincennes

The party walked a short way to a low embankment on the grounds, where twelve French soldiers awaited the group. When stood in front of a small mound, a French officer offered Father Arbaux a white cloth to blindfold her. Marguerite immediately inquired if the blindfold was necessary. The officer replied no. Marguerite stood facing the firing squad unbound and stared at the soldiers. As the officer's sword fell the soldiers fired in mass. Marguerite fell in an erect fashion and lay back facing towards the sky. Following French Army protocol, a sergeant walked up to the body, drew his pistol, and shot the alleged German spy in the head. Thus, ended the intriguing and tragic life of the woman we know today as Mata Hari.

Born on August 7, 1876 in Leeuwarden, Holland, Mata Hari, whose real name was Marguerite Gertrude Zelle, had a Dutch father and mother. She grew up in a middle-class environment, but after her father's remarriage and the death of her mother, Marguerite found herself poor and living with an uncle in The Hague. In 1895, to escape a hopeless future, Marguerite became a mail-order bride and married a Dutch army captain, Rudolf MacLeod, who lived in the Dutch East Indies. Her marriage proved to be a disaster, as MacLeod was a physically abusive alcoholic. They had two children, a son Norman and a daughter Jeanne. In 1899, Norman died tragically of food poisoning. In March 1902, after MacLeod retired from the Dutch army, the family returned to Holland with their marriage in shambles. Marguerite and MacLeod separated in August with Marguerite obtaining custody of their daughter. Months later MacLeod abducted Jeanne and kept her illegally until she died suddenly at the age of twenty-one. Marguerite Zelle was alone and destitute.

The next year, Marguerite moved to Paris with her lover, Baron Henry de Marguérie, a minor Dutch diplomat. Bright and resourceful, she tried to earn a living as a model, and then as a riding instructor and circus rider. She failed. Baron Marguérie suggested dancing. Traditionally, this meant as a dance hall dancer, but Marguerite thought to reinvent herself as an exotic Indian dancer. At a time when modern dance was evolving and becoming popular due to celebrities such as Isadora Duncan, Marguerite became an immediate success. In the audience for her first performance, she took the name Lady MacLeod, pitching herself as the half Indian wife of a British aristocrat.

At that performance her soon-to-be lover, industrialist Émile Étienne Guimet, founder of the Musée Guimet in Paris, was immediately taken with her. Guimet set the stage for Marguerite's first performance as Mata Hari. He thought Marguerite needed a stage name. Marguerite already had one in mind from her time spent in the Dutch Indies, Mata Hari, which in Malayalam means, "the light of day or dawn." Mata Hari's first public performance was presented in what now is the Guimet museum. After this successful performance Mata Hari had the good fortune to team up with Gabriel Astruc, the most influential stage manager and promoter during the Belle Époque. Her career, spanning from 1905 to 1915, placed Mata Hari into the highest social circles of Europe.

Entrance to the donjon of the Château de Vincennes

In 1914 at the onset of World War I, Mata Hari found her career as an exotic dancer waning and her life slipping into the role of a famed courtesan. When Germany entered the war on August 4, 1914, Mata Hari was dancing in Berlin. She returned to Holland. She acquired a new lover, the Marquis de Beaufort, a Belgian officer stationed at the front, with whom she continued a long-term on-and-off relationship.

Acquiring new Dutch and French passports, Mata Hari attempted to return to Paris and be with de Beaufort, but because of the war, direct rail to Paris was impossible with the Germans occupying most of Belgium. Given her career history both British and French secret services were showing interest in this famous dancer who, at the outbreak of the war, was living in Berlin and having a part time affair with a German policeman. After returning to Paris in June 1916, via neutral Spain, the British secret service warned French police of Mata Hari's return. French intelligence assigned two counter espionage agents to follow her. When Mata Hari met up with the Marquis de Beaufort in July, Mata Hari promptly complained to Paris police that she was being followed, hardly the response of a professional spy.

Mata Hari now met the love of her life, a Russian volunteering in the French army, twenty-one-year-old Vladimir de Masloff; she was forty. Masloff was terribly wounded losing an eye and held at a hospital in Vittel, France. Marguerite, wishing to see her lover, went to the French authorities, to get a special pass to visit Masloff. Mata Hari was sent, unbeknownst to her, to a Georges Ladoux, head of French counter espionage. British officials from Scotland Yard Special Branch had told Ladoux that Mata Hari could be a German spy having the code name AF-44. It was a case of mistaken identity. At this meeting Ladoux proposed to Mata Hari that she think about spying for France. The offer was made with the clear knowledge from the British that Mata Hari was already working for the Germans. Completely innocent of her situation, Mata Hari agreed to spy for France because she was desperately in need of money. Ladox hired her on a trial basis.

In November 1916 Ladoux decided to post Mata Hari to occupied Brussels. The route was again circuitous because of the war. She traveled through neutral Spain with a stopover first in Falmouth, England as the British were inspecting all ships leaving France. When her ship docked Mata Hari was held and taken to London. Sir Basil Thomson, head of Special Branch Scotland Yard, the counter espionage group for Britain, wrongly believed Mata Hari to be the known German spy, Clara Benedix. Declaring her innocence and true identity, Mata Hari was permitted to continue her journey to Spain, with the eventual goal of reaching Belgium.

In December Mata Hari was held up in Madrid, and at the suggestion of Ladoux, she tried to contact German intelligence officials. Eventually, Mata Hari got an appointment with a Captain Arnold Kalle, a German intelligence officer stationed in Madrid. At that meeting Kalle already suspected Mata Hari of being a French intelligence agent, but he decided to hear Mata Hari's proposal that she work for the German government. Kalle agreed and sent Marguerite back to Paris. She never reached Belgium.

Mata Hari arrived in Paris on January 4, 1917 and reported to Ladoux, expecting to be rewarded and hired full time as a French spy. Marguerite informed Ladoux about her discussions with Captain Kalle in Madrid. Again, Ladoux assigned two French agents to follow her. Another event earlier in Paris sealed Mata Hari's fate.

One of the reasons for the survival of Gustav Eiffel's tower was its use as a listening post during World War I. Radio communications were line-of-sight, and the Eiffel Tower made it possible for French agents to listen to radio messages deep inside Germany. On December 13, 1916, a German message was intercepted at the Eiffel Tower revealing a German spy codenamed H-21. When this message was given to Ladoux, he believed H-21 must be Mata Hari. Most importantly, if Mata Hari was in fact H-21, she must have gotten that codename before her trip to Madrid. Mata Hari had to be a German spy. The Germans purposely had sent this message, pertaining to H-21, to deceive French intelligence.

Without any definitive evidence to detain Mata Hari, Ladoux went ahead and arrested her on February 13, 1917, and charged her with spying for Germany. French authorities claimed in the arrest that Mata Hari was responsible for the deaths of over fifty thousand Allied soldiers. Her trial began on July 24, 1917. The trial or more properly a military tribunal was a shameful reflection of the moment. Mata Hari's attorney was denied the right to cross-examine witnesses, nor allowed his own witnesses to testify on her behalf. Some evidence against her was clearly fabricated. Mata Hari was a made-to-order scapegoat at a time in the war when France's fortunes were going poorly. Given the mutinies in the French Army during 1917, the government was desperate for small victories.

Convicted on all charges Mata Hari was executed on October 15, 1917 on the park grounds of the Bois de Vincennes. France had Marguerite's estate pay for the trial and her execution. With no family to claim the corpse, the body was given to the University of Paris. Eventually her decapitated cadaver disappeared.

Five days before the liberation of Paris German soldiers of the Waffen-SS rounded up twenty-six French policemen and Resistance fighters on August 20, 1944. The Germans immediately executed them along the eastern wall of the Vincennes fortress and threw the corpses into a mass unmarked grave.

How to get there: Two metro stops serve the Bois de Vincennes and the Château de Vincennes. Metro station Château de Vincennes is close to the château-fortress and Park Floral, which is adjacent to the fortress complex. Metro station Porte-Dorée is located next to the main entrance to the park and Lake Daumesnil.

It is a long walk from the center of Paris to the Bois de Vincennes, but my wife and I have made the journey on several occasions. Begin at the Place de Bastille, follow the Rue de Lyon until the street becomes the Avenue Daumesnil. Avenue Daumesnil will take you to the entrance to the Bois de Vincennes near the Port Dorée metro station. This route allows you to walk through the Promenade Plantée (also known as the Coulée verte René-Dumont), an elevated city garden built on top of an old rail line entering Paris. This walk is unique and one of my favorites. Enjoy summer flowers with a stroll through the Parc Floral.

Walkway through Promenade Plantée

Parc Floral

Chapter 19. Jardins du Ranelagh

"Three may keep a secret, if two of them are dead." (1)
Benjamin Franklin (1706–1790)

The Jardins du Ranelagh is a quiet unobtrusive park in the affluent neighborhood of Passy. Like many of the smaller parks in Paris, nearby residents are the principal visitors. During the summer months the gardens accommodate lunch groups of neighboring workers from the La Muette metro area. Art lovers visiting the Musée Marmottan Monet have probably walked through Ranelagh Gardens not knowing its name or its relationship to a momentous event in history.

The gardens are named after the Ranelagh Gardens in London. Richard Jones, the first Earl of Ranelagh, built a rococo rotunda for music concerts in 1689 on the grounds of the Chelsea Hospital in London. In 1772 two representatives of King Louis XV were visiting London, saw the Ranelagh Gardens and its music hall, and returned to France with the idea of building a similar rotunda in Paris. In 1774 the city selected a location on the grounds of the Château de la Muette and built a concert hall with a café and restaurant. They named the new gardens the Le Petit Ranelagh. Frequented by Marie-Antoinette and Louis XVI's brother, the Count d'Artois, the dance hall was fashionable with the court. Though popular through the Napoleonic Wars and the Restoration, the hall was torn down in 1858. In 1860 Baron Haussmann, as part of the renovation of Paris, created the park we enjoy today on the grounds of the original Château de la Muette. Our story begins six years before the French Revolution and tells the tale of two brothers who made paper for a living.

"Accordingly, Mr. Stryver inaugurated the Long Vacation with a formal proposal to take Miss Manette to Vauxhall Hall Gardens; that failing, to Ranelagh...", A Tale of Two Cities by Charles Dickens (1859)

November 21, 1783: Pilâtre de Rozier and the Marquis d'Arlandes become the first humans to leave the Earth in free flight.

In the fall of 1782, France and England had been at war for several years with France supporting the American Revolution. Frenchman Joseph-Michel Montgolfier was living in Avignon and enjoying life as a successful paper manufacturer. One evening Joseph-Michel was daydreaming about how French forces could attack the impregnable British fortress of Gibraltar. Since the fort was immune from attacks by land and sea, Joseph fantasized how an aerial assault might be accomplished.

A summer afternoon in the Jardins du Ranelagh

Sitting in the kitchen Joseph noticed how the heated air from the kitchen stove filled loose wet pants that were hanging above and cause their legs to rise. Joseph reasoned that a special gas from the fire gave the gas the property of lift and thus ballooning up his drying pants legs. Based on this observation his first experiment involved the construction of a small wooden box slightly less than a square meter sealed with taffeta cloth. When a small fire of crushed paper was lit inside the box, it immediately flew into the air and sailed away. Montgolfier was astonished. With the assistance of his brother, Jacques-Étienne Montgolfier, Joseph built a much larger box approximately three times the size of the first one. On December 14, 1782 the Montgolfier brothers successfully launched their first hot-air unmanned balloon. The flight covered approximately one mile. The brothers' balloon development continued through 1783 with the assistance of Jean-Baptiste Réveillon. Réveillon lived in Paris and made high quality wallpaper which was much stronger than printing paper. By adding a superficial coating of an alum mixture, Réveillon's paper and taffeta were more resistant to burn. The three men built the Aérostat Réveillon, flown for the first time on September 19, 1783, which carried a sheep, a rooster, and a duck. The brothers were concerned that flight above the ground might injure a person. The flight was performed at the Palace of Versailles in the presence of Louis XVI and his court with great fanfare. The animals' flight reached an altitude of fifteen hundred feet and covered a distance of nearly two miles. The next step was to build a balloon large enough for human flight.

In the Faubourg Saint-Antoine district, at Réveillon's shop, the brothers built a new balloon having a height of seventy-five feet and a diameter of roughly fifty feet. In was now ready for human flight. While tethered to the ground Jacques-Étienne made the first ascent to a height of about fifty to eighty feet. Physicist and professor Jean-François Pilâtre de Rozier, assisted with the work and became the second aeronaut to fly in the tethered balloon. Louis XVI forbade any free flights due to his perception of the danger. Rozier's friends, close to the king, were finally able to obtain Louis XVI's permission to attempt an untethered flight. Louis stipulated that for such an historical moment, the aeronauts must be of noble rank. Therefore, an old school friend of Joseph Montgolfier, the Marquis François le Vieux d'Arlandes, volunteered for the first flight.

On November 21, 1783, 1:54 p.m., a huge crowd of Parisians gathered to watch the first ascent of man into the sky on the grounds of the Château de la Muette, where the present Ranelagh Gardens now reside. The two aeronauts were professor Rozier and the Marquis d'Arlandes. The Marquis noted in his journal that after stoking the fire with straw he yelled to Rozier, "This time we are rising!" Leaving the grounds of the villa, the balloon drifted at first over the village of Passy, then down the Seine past the Invalides. Huge crowds throughout Paris screamed in astonishment. Traveling past the cathedral of Saint-Sulpice and the Luxembourg Gardens, the Marquis had to sponge off tiny holes developing in the balloon due to burning embers floating up into the fabric. After coming close to hitting the blades of two windmills the balloon settled down in the neighborhood of Butte-aux-Cailles. The flight lasted a half an hour. The Jardin de la Montgolfière, a park in the thirteenth arrondissement, commemorates the landing site. Benjamin Franklin, American envoy to France, witnessed the flight with great admiration. Paris became the first aerostation on Earth.

Benjamin Franklin lived in the village of Passy, adjacent to the Château de la Muette, from 1776 to 1785 as the representative of the United States to the court of Louis XVI. During his time in Passy Franklin managed a small printing business to propagandize America's efforts in the American Revolution. Franklin published comics called "Bagatelles" and many philosophical and scientific articles. Living close to the Seine Franklin was a frequent swimmer during the summer months.

How to get there: The closest metro station to the Jardins du Ranglegh is La Muette, located at the intersection of Chausée de la Muette and Rue François Ponsard. Upon leaving the metro station, walk westward towards the Bois de Boulogne. The entrance to the gardens begins, where the street bifurcates into the Avenue Ingres on your left and Avenue Prudhon on your right.

One of the smaller and less visited museums in Paris because of its location in the sixteenth arrondissement, is the Musée du Marmottan Monet. Located at No. 2 Rue Louis Boilly, the museum was a gift of Paul Marmottan to the French Academy of Fine Arts in 1934. The museum houses an extensive collection of paintings by Claude Monet, which was a gift from Monet's second son, Michel Monet in 1966.

The sixteenth arrondissement has the top sports palaces in Paris. Tennis enthusiasts fill the Roland Garros Stadium to watch the French Open. Followers of the Paris Saint-Germain professional football club watch the home team at the Parc des Princes, while rugby followers fill the Stade Jean-Bouin. On Sunday April 27, 1857, the Emperor Napoleon III and his wife Eugénie opened the Hippodrome de Longchamp, which can accommodate up to fifty thousand spectators.

Chapter 20. Bois de Boulogne and the Château de Bagatelle

"Courage! I have shown it for years; think you I shall lose it at the moment when my sufferings are to end?" (1) Marie-Antoinette (1755–1793)

The Bois de Boulogne is a collage of attractions. Enjoy walking through a woodland? There are miles of footpaths. During the week the Bois is relatively quiet, but Saturdays and Sundays sees locals everywhere enjoying the greenery. One autumn afternoon my wife and I were walking along a path and watched a pheasant scratching her way through a bed of fallen leaves searching for insects. Children enjoy the amusement park in the Jardin d'Acclimatation with its zoo and carnival rides. The rose garden of the Château de Bagatelle and the green houses at the Jardin des serres d'Auteuil delight any home gardener or flower lover. The Foundation Louis Vuitton, a contemporary art museum and cultural center, is the newest addition to the Bois. Designed by Frank Gehry, the building is a major attraction in itself with spectacular veranda views of La Défense and the Bois.

Let us begin our histories with the Romans. The Bois was first named Roburitum in Roman Gaul, which became Rovertum, then Rouveret, and finally Rouvray in medieval centuries. In 717 Chilpéric II gave, "the forest of Rouvray situated amongst the Parisi tribe along the Seine", to the Abbey de Saint-Denis. In 1109 the abbey sold the western area of the forest to King Phillip II to be used as a hunting preserve. The shrine to the Virgin Mary in the town of Boulogne-sur-Mer so inspired King Philip IV that he built a similar shrine in the Bois, hence the modern name Bois de Boulogne.

The name of the Hippodrome de Longchamp originates from the Franciscan Abbey of Longchamp, which Isabelle of France founded in 1255. The Abbey was located in the Bois de Boulogne near the site of the track.

Paths through the Bois de Boulogne with skyscrapers in the La Defense area of Paris

1527: Francis I constructs the Château de Madrid, The House of Mistresses.

How did this impressive château acquire the name Château de Madrid? Francis I, the Renaissance king and patron of Leonardo de Vinci, was leading French armies in the Four Years War against the Holy Roman Emperor Charles V. The two monarchs hated one another. Disregarding the warnings of his generals about the monarch's risky behavior on the battlefield, Francis was insistent and foolhardy. Philip's Basque and Spanish troops captured the French king at the Battle of Pavia on February 24, 1525. Francis was immediately taken to Madrid and held captive in the Royal Alcázar Palace. After signing the Treaty of Madrid, which made large concessions to Charles V, Francis I was released on March 17, 1526.

Returning to Paris, Francis disliked living in the cold dark Louvre Palace. The king built a new Renaissance palace at the edge of the Bois de Boulogne, which he named appropriately the Château de Boulogne., The palace unofficially acquired the name Château de Madrid because of Francis's lengthy imprisonment in Madrid.

For reasons that are obscure today, Francis I never lived in the Château de Madrid. The palace became home to a series of mistresses. Francis I's mistress, Anna de Pisseleu d'Heilly, Duchess of Étampes was the first resident. When Francis I died, Henry II replaced Anna with his own mistress, Diane de Poitiers. Charles IX, keeping the tradition, installed his mistress, Marie Touchet in the palace. Henry IV, kept several mistresses in the château. One of them was Henriette d'Entragues, the daughter of Marie Touchet.

During the following centuries the Château de Madrid lost favor with the monarchy and the palace faded into ruins. During the Revolution the edifice was sold to a demolition contractor who lost money in tearing it down. A few of the beautiful glazed tiles, which adorned the exterior, were saved and now reside in the city museum of Paris, the Musée Carnivalet.

When the famous opera diva, Catherine-Nicole Le Maure (1704–1786), retired to the Abbey de Longchamp, she held concerts in the Abbey. Parisians, including the nobility, flocked to Catherine's performances to the degree that the archbishop of Paris had to close the abbey to the public to preserve the abbey's reputation.

March 1719: Duel between the Marquise de Nesle and the Countess de Polignac

Louis du Plessis, the Duke de Richelieu (the great-nephew of Cardinal de Richelieu), was a ladies-man extraordinaire. One of his biographers, Hubert Cole, named the Duke, the "First Gentleman of the Bedchamber." At times his rascally sexual behavior led to trouble and the following entertaining moment still reverberates through the centuries. Jean Buvat, in his *Journal de Régence* 1715–1723, on the date of March 14, 1719, told our tale. The Duke's secretary accidently scheduled a clandestine meeting with two of his mistresses at the same time and place. His paramours were the Marquise de Nesle, daughter of the Duke de Mazarin, and her sister-in-law, Madame de Polignac, daughter of the Count of Mailly. After a brief, but physically violent scuffle, the two agreed to meet in the Bois de Boulogne in a duel with pistols.

On the agreed upon day in the Bois the two women were at first separated to a distance. A white scarf was dropped signaling for them to walk toward each other, with pistols at the ready, and allowed to fire at each other whenever it suited them. As they began pacing towards each other, Madame de Polignac shouted out, "You fire first, and don't miss, if you believe I'll miss you!" The completely rattled Marquise de Nesle wildly aimed and fired first, hitting a nearby tree. Madame de Polignac, took careful aim, fired, and watched the Marquise fall to the ground in a pool of blood. Fortunately, the Marquise was only slightly wounded in the shoulder and fully recovered. Afterwards the Duke dumped the winner, Madame de Polignac, and continued his relationship with the loser, the Marquise de Nesle. Perhaps the Duke thought it too venturesome to have a mistress proficient with a handgun.

Most duels portrayed in Hollywood films are incorrect. Duelers were first separated at some agreed upon distance and stood facing each other. When a white scarf was dropped between them, they were then told to start walking towards each other.

Duelers were allowed to shoot of their own volition while walking towards each other. This procedure prevented cheating.

Château des Îles in the Bois de Boulogne

November 26, 1777: The Count d'Artois wins a bet with Marie-Antoinette by building the Château de Bagatelle in less than ninety days.

Victor Marie d'Estrées, the Duke of Estrées built a small hunting lodge at the edge of the Bois in 1720. In 1775 Louis XVI's brother, the Count d'Artois and the future King Charles X, purchased the land and leveled the old building to prepare for a new more luxurious weekend retreat. The Count commissioned François-Joseph Bélanger to build a relatively small neoclassical villa with accompanying gardens. The Count named the villa, the Château de Bagatelle. The word bagatelle comes from the Italian word, *bagattella* meaning, "a triviality." Just prior to the construction, Marie-Antoinette bet the Count that the château could not be completed in less than three months. Determined, the Count assigned approximately eight hundred workers to toil day and night beginning on September 21, 1777. The château was completed on November 26. A Latin engraving over the portico reads, *Parvus sed aptus*, meaning, "humble, but sufficient."

> *At parties Marie-Antoinette and the Count played a game, which the Count nicknamed, bagatelle. It was played on an inclined table with ridged sides. A player, using a cue-like stick, pushed ivory balls up the incline trying to avoid vertical pins set on the table with the aim of landing the balls down into holes on the table's surface. The game eventually became popular throughout Europe. After many mechanical and electronic innovations over two centuries bagatelle evolved into the modern pinball machine.*

June 5, 1896: Anna Gould celebrates her twenty first birthday in the Bois de Boulogne.

If you have forgotten what life was like before income tax, read about Anna Gould's birthday party. The daughter of railroad financier, Jay Gould, Anna Gould could afford an ostentatious birthday party, but the Gould gala was acutely emblematic of the Gilded Age. Held in the Bois de Boulogne, Anna's twenty-first birthday party featured the entire Paris Opera Company and a two-hundred-piece orchestra. Eighty thousand Venetian lanterns lit the path over the fifteen kilometers of red velvet carpeting. Two hundred torchbearers further lighted up the grounds. The reception held two hundred fifty dinner guests, while later approximately 3,000 attendees enjoyed the concert. At the end of the festivity's fireworks lit the sky, while two hundred terrified swans were released into Lac Inférieur.

Anna married Paul "Boni" Boniface de Castellane. She brought a thirteen-million-dollar purse to shore up the Castellane family fortunes. However, after five children and Paul spending all of Anna's money, the couple divorced with international notoriety in 1906.

October 23, 1906: Pioneer Brazilian aviator, Alberto Santos-Dumont flies the first heavier-than-air aircraft in Europe on the grounds of the Château de Bagatelle.

Born the last of seven children to a wealthy coffee plantation family in Palmira, Brazil, Alberto Santos-Dumont, spent most of his adult life in Paris. A brilliant aviator, Santos-Dumont first became known for flying airships. He won the Deutsch de la Meurthe prize on October 19, 1901 for flying a dirigible round-trip from the Park Saint-Cloud to the Eiffel Tower in less than thirty minutes. Ever the dandy, Alberto peddled his small No. 9 dirigible into central Paris and parked it on the street like an automobile.

On October 23, 1906 Santos-Dumont flew the first powered airplane in Europe on the lawns of the Château de Bagatelle. Santos-Dumont's model, Demoiselle No. 19, became the world's first mass-produced aircraft. Approximately fifty aircraft were built from a planned production of one hundred.

> *Santos-Dumont found it difficult to check the time with his pocket watch while piloting his aircraft which required the use of both hands. He went to his good friend Louis Cartier and asked if he could design a watch easily read. In 1904 Cartier developed one of the world's first wristwatches. Cartier still sells several models of the Santos-Dumont wristwatch.*

James Abbott McNeill Whistler, American artist and famous raconteur during the Belle Époque, idled away afternoons playing pétanque in the Bois de Boulogne.

Author Richard De Gallienne, visiting the Bagatelle in 1936, wrote that the dairy milked the cows every day at four o' clock. Visitors either took afternoon tea at the Goûter de Bagatelle, or dinner at the upscale Restaurant du Château de Madrid. Gallienne made special note of the rose garden and water lilies in the pond, which still thrive today.

Peacocks at the Château de Bagatelle

On August 14, 1944 the German Army rounded up thirty-five young men from Resistance groups in Paris and took them to the Bois de Boulogne near the Longchamps hippodrome. The Frenchmen were lined up, gunned down, and dumped in a common grave.

Jardin d'Acclimatation

How to get there: The Bois de Boulogne is located on the western edge of Paris in the sixteenth arrondissement. The Seine borders the park's western side and the Boulevard Périphérique borders its eastern side.

Due to the size of the Bois, several metro and RER trains serve the Bois de Boulogne. At the southern end of the park near the Jardin des serres d'Auteuil and the hippodrome is the metro station Port d'Auteuil. Further north is the metro station La Muette that lies near the entrance of the Jardins du Ranelagh, which in turn, adjoins up to the border of the Bois. Entering the Bois from La Muette will lead to the walking paths around the Lac Supérieur and Lac Inférieur. Metro and RER station Gare de Neuilly - Porte Maillot is the closest for visiting the Jardin d' Acclimatation, the Foundation Louis Vuitton, or the Château de Bagatelle. Also, if walking from the two lakes area bus 244 runs along Allée de Longchamps, which stops near the afore mentioned attractions.

Chapter 21 Chronology

The date of creation for each park has been inserted into the Chronology according to *Les Parcs et Jardins de Paris: 400 lieux de détente et de decouverte* by Sabine Jeanin (2001, Rustica Edition). These dates reflect when the city of Paris officially established the current park or garden.

c. 250 BC   Parisii clan of the Celtic tribe Senones settle on islands in the Seine.

52 BC   General Labienus, a lieutenant of Julius Caesar, defeats the Parisii.

1st century   Romans construct the Arènes de Lutèce.

508   Clovis I establishes Paris as his capital.

1163   Work begins on the cathedral of Notre Dame.

1190   Philip II Augustus begins construction of the Louvre Palace.

1254   Knights Templar complete Temple fortress in Paris.

1257   The Sorbonne school opens.

c. 1410   Valois kings complete the Chateau de Vincennes.

1429   Joan of Arc campaigns with the French armies.

1515–1547   Reign of Francis I

1547–1559   Reign of Henry II

1572   Catherine de Medici completes the Tuileries Palace and Garden.

1572   Catholics murder Protestants during the Saint Bartholomew's Day massacre.

1594–1610   Reign of Henry IV

1612   The Jardin du Luxembourg opens.

1633   Jardins du Palais-Royal opens.

1635   Cardinal Richelieu establishes the Académie Français.

1635   Current Jardin des Plantes opens.

1644   Jardin des Tuileries (official recognition)

1643–1715   Louis XIV reigns as King of France and begins construction of the Palace of Versailles.

1677–1682   Affair of the Poisons

1682   Place des Vosges (Square Louis-XIII) opens.

1720   Esplanade des Invalides opens.

1715–1774   The reign of Louis XV

1774   Louis XVI crowned King of France.

1781   Louis Philippe II completes the expansion of the Palais-Royal.

1783   The Treaty of Paris ends the American Revolution.

1789   Parisians storm the Bastille prison. French Revolution begins.

1792   French First Republic

1793   Louis XVI is guillotined at the Place de la Révolution.

1795   Paris divides the city into twelve governmental arrondissements.

1804   Napoleon Bonaparte crowned Emperor of France.

1815   Napoleon Bonaparte is defeated at the Battle of Waterloo.

1830   Louis-Philippe ascends the throne of France during July Revolution.

1840   Jardins des Champs-Élysées and Promenade du Cours-la-Reine open.

1848   February Revolution establishes the Second Republic.

1851   Napoleon III establishes the Second Empire.

1853   Prefect of the Seine, Baron George Haussmann begins the complete renovation of Paris.

1856   Square de la Tour Saint-Jacques opens.

1857   Square du Temple opens.

1858   Bois de Boulogne opens.

1859   Square Louvois opens.

1860   Bois de Vincennes and Jardins du Ranelagh open.

1861   Parc Monceau opens.

1863   Édouard Manet's, *Déjeuner sur l'herbe*, highlights the Salon des Refusés (Salon of Rejects), which opened at the Palais de l'Industrie.

1870   French Third Republic

1871   Franco-Prussian War ends. Communards revolt in Paris.

1875   The Opéra Garnier opens.

1884   Square du Vert-Galant opens.

1889   The World's Fair of 1889 debuts the Eiffel Tower.

1892   Square des Arénes de Lutèce et Square Capitan opens.

1900   World's Fair of 1900 sees the construction of the Pont Alexander III, the Grand Palais, and the Petit Palais.

1908   Parc du Champ-de-Mars opens.

1914   Assassination of Archduke Franz Ferdinand in Sarajevo marks the start of World War I. The aerial bombing of Paris begins.

1918   Armistice signed ending World War One.

1926   Jardin du musée Carnavalet opens.

1927   Charles Lindbergh completes first transatlantic crossing by air from New York to Paris.

1939   Nazis Germany invades Poland starting World War Two.

1944   On August 25 Paris is liberated from German occupation.

1945   World War Two ends.

1946   French Fourth Republic

1948   Marshall Plan initiated to assist European recovery from World War Two.

1958   French Fifth Republic, Work begins on the the La Défense business district.

1959–1969   General Charles de Galle is President of France.

1962   Algeria wins its independence from France.

1968   Students riot in France over living conditions and students' rights.

1970   Square de la place Dauphine opens.

2000   Jardin medieval du musée de Cluny reopens.

Chapter 22 Source Notes

"While in Paris … to look at it.", Jefferson, Thomas. Index of The Memoirs, Correspondence, And Miscellanies, from The Papers of Thomas Jefferson, Edited by Thomas Jefferson Randolph. 1829. Index compiled by David Widger, Project Gutenberg Editions, EBook #28860.

Jardins du Palais-Royal

1 "What is this world? A complex whole, subject to endless revolutions." Denis Diderot, Lettre sur les aveugles (Letter on the Blind, 1749), Morley, John. Diderot And the Encyclopædists, Vol. II., London and New York: Macmillan And Co., Limited, 1905.

2 "I have killed one man to save a hundred thousand." At Charlott's trial for the assassination of Jean-Paul Marat [1743-1793] [July 1793], Du Bois, Louis. Charlotte de Corday: essai historique, offrant enfin des détails authentiques sur la personne et l'attentat de cette heroine, Paris: Librairie Historique de la Révolution, 1838.

3 "Dans ce jardin on ne rencontre" Jacques Abbé Delille, Les Jardins, en quatre chants, 1780, from Oeuvres Completed De Jacques Delille, Bruxelles: J. Maubach, 1817.

4 "The pamphlet shops … the Palais-Royal!", Young, Arthur. Travels in France during the Years 1787, 1788, 1789, Franklin Classics (2018, Matilda Betham-Edwards), 1792.

5 "In six minutes… the astonished multitude.", Sébastien-Roch, Nicolas. Œuvres completes de Chamfort, recueillies et publiées, avec une notice historique sur la vie et les écrits de l'auteur, par p. r. auguis., tome premier. paris. chez chaumerot jeune, libraire, palais-royal, galeries de bois, no 189. 1824.

6 "Rumour, therefore… be on fire!", Carlyle, Thomas. The French Revolution: A History, 1837. Project Gutenberg eBook #1301.

7 "All seemed quiet… what they wanted." Blaikie, Thomas. Diary of a Scotch Gardener at the French Court at the End of the Eighteenth Century, Ed. And Introduction by Francis Birrell, London: George Routledge and Sons, Ltd. 1931.

James Bowers

8 "I spent five days… the précis of Paris.", Mercier, Louis-Sébastien. Le Tableau de Paris 1782-1788, 12 Vol. Translated and abridged into English by Helen Simpson, Philadelphia: J. B. Lippincott Co., 1933.

9 "The Palais-Royal… had its own hall." Siboutie, de la Poumiès. Recollections of a Parisian (Docteur Poumiès de la Siboutie) Under Six Sovereigns, Two Revolutions,and a Republic (1789–1863), Eds. Mesdames A. Branche and L. Dagoury, Translated by Lady Theodora Davidson, London: John Murray, 1911.

10 "I have been… met a like fate." Siboutie, de la Poumiès. Recollections of a Parisian (Docteur Poumiès de la Siboutie) Under Six Sovereigns, Two Revolutions,and a Republic (1789–1863), Eds. Mesdames A. Branche and L. Dagoury, Translated by Lady Theodora Davidson, London: John Murray,. 1911.

11 "The true traveler is he who goes on foot, and even then, he sits down a lot of the time." Colette, Sidonie-Gabrielle. Paris de ma fenêtre, Geneva: Editions du Milieu du Monde, 1944.

12 "To a poet, silence is an acceptable response, even a flattering one." Colette, Sidonie-Gabrielle. Paris de ma fenêtre, Geneva: Editions du Milieu du Monde, 1944.

Jardin des Tuileries

1 "The word impossible is not French." Letter to General Jean Le Marois (July 9, 1813), quoted in Latham, Edward. Famous Sayings and their Authors: A Collection of Historical Sayings in English, French, German, Greek, Italian, And Latin, London: Swan Sonnenschein and Co. Lim. 1906.

2 "But the nobility… Or foes to strike with terror;" Wright, Elizur. The Battle of the Rats and the Weasels, New Edition with notes, London: J. W. M. Gibbs 1882.

3 "And now… Rue de Rivoli", Thackeray William Makepeace. *The Paris Sketch Book of Mr. M. A. Titmarsh*, London: MacMillan and Company, 1902.

Square du Vert Galant

1 "J me porte comme le Pont-Neuf.": Le Gallienne, Richard. From a Paris Garret, Ives New York: Washburn Publisher, 1936.

2 "O, you Pont-Neuf… Pickpocket.": Ibid.

Square Louvois

1 "Et tu Brute?": Shakespeare William, Julius Caesar (Act III, Scene I), 1623.

Square de la Place Dauphine

1 "And how,": Mercier, Louis-Sébastien. Le Tableau de Paris 1782-1788, 12 Vol. Translated and abridged into English by Helen Simpson, Philadelphia: J. B. Lippincott Co., 1933.

Square du Temple

1 "Templar is… demons nor men.": Mabillon, Dom. Joannes. *The Complete Works of Saint Bernard, Abbot of Clairvaux*, translated by Dr. Samuel John Eales, London: John Hodges, 1904.

Jardin du Musée Carnavalet

1 "There is no person who is not dangerous for someone.": Roberts, Kate Louise. Hoyt's New Cyclopedia of Practical Quotations, New York And London: Funk & Wagnalls Company, 1922.

2 "Thank god we… beautiful neighborhood.": Rabutin-Chantal, Marie de. Lettres De Mme de Sévigné, Précédées d'une notice sur sa vie et du traité sur le style épistolaire de Madame de Sévigné, par M. Suard,secrétaire perpétuel de l'académie française, paris, librairie de firmin didot freres, Imprimeurs de l'institut, Rue jacob, 56, 1846. The author's translation.

3 "Ingratitude calls forth reproaches as gratitude brings renewed kindnesses.": Roberts, Kate Louise. Hoyt's New Cyclopedia of Practical Quotations, New York And London: Funk & Wagnalls Company, 1922.

4 "I am going to tell you… the truth or not.": Aldis, Janet. The Queen of Letter-Writers, London: Metheun and Co. and New York: G. P. Putnam's Sons. 1907.

5 "On Saturday… : Aldis, Janet. The Queen of Letter-Writers, London: Metheun and Co. and New York: G. P. Putnam's Sons. 1907.

6 "Quelle femme… et l'esprit.": Aldis, Janet. The Queen of Letter-Writers, London: Metheun and Co. and New York: G. P. Putnam's Sons. 1907.

Tour St. Jacques

1 "I have made… make it shorter.": Tulloch, Principal. Pascal, Provincial Letters: Letter XVI (4 December 1656), Edinburgh and London: William Blackwood And Sons, 1878.—reprint, 1882.

Place des Vosges

1 "I will be Chateaubriand or nothing.": Pellissier, Georges. The Literary Movement in France During the Nineteenth Century, Authorized English Version by Ann Garrison Brinton, New York and London: G. P. Putnams Sons, 1897.

2 "While we are … you desire more?": Rabutin, Bussy. Histoire Amoureuse Des Gaules, Suivie des Romans historico-satiriques du XVIIe siècle, Tome 1,2, &3, recueillis et annotés par M. C.-L. Livet, Paris: Chez P. Jannet, Libraire, 1856.

Le Jardin des Arènes de Lutèce

1 "Do not trust the horse, Trojans. Whatever it is, I fear the Greeks even when they bring gifts.": Virgil. *The Aeneid Of Virgil*, Translated into English by J. W. Mackail, M.A., London: Macmillan And Co., 1885.

Jardin des Plantes

1 "We will now… for existence.": Darwin, Charles. On the Origin of Species. Or the Preservation of Favored Races in the Struggle for Life, From the First Edition, London: John Murray, 1859.

Jardin du Musée de Cluny

1 "Veni, vidi, vici.": Inscription on the triumphal wagon reported in The Twelve Caesars by Suetonius.

2 "Winding far down… throned on torsoes!": Melville, Herman. Moby Dick or The Whale, New York: Harper and Brothers, 1851.

Jardin du Luxembourg

1 "There is nothing left because if it were left it would be left over.": Stein, Gertrude. *Geography and Plays*, Boston: The Four Seas Co. Publ. 1922.

2 "Masterpieces are only lucky attempts.": Sand, George. François le Champi; Jane Minot Sedgwick (trans.) François the Waif. New York: H. M. Caldwell, 1894.

3 "Tous pour un, un pour tous, c'est notre devise.":Dumas, Alexander. Les Trois Mousquetaires. Published in the journal Le Siècle from March to July, 1844.

4 "You look ridiculous... as well dance.": Stein, Gertrude. Three Lives.,New York: Grafton Press, 1909.

Esplanade des Invalides

1 "There are only two forces that unite men — fear and interest.": Bonaparte, Napoleon. Napoleon: In His Own Words, From the French of Jules Bertaut, Translated by H. E. Law and C. L. Rhodes, Chicago: A. C. McClurg and Co., 1916.

2 "I went out... on the battlefield.": Perris, George. The Battle of the Marne, London: Methuen and Co. Ltd., 1920.

Parc du Champ-de-mars

1 "Mr. Watson. Come here. I want to see you.": Bell, Alexander Graham. First intelligible words spoken over the telephone (10 March 1876), The Library of Congress, The Alexander Graham Bell Family Papers, Notebook by Alexander Graham Bell, from 1875 to 1876.

2 "Citizens, did you want a revolution without a revolution?": Réponse à J.- B. Louvet, a speech to the National Convention on November 5, 1792.

Jardins des Champs-Elysées-Reine

1 "La vie est la farce à mener par tous.": Rimbaud, Artur. Une Saison en Enfer. Bruxelles: Alliance Typographique (M.-J. Poot et Compagnie), 1873.

Parc Monceau

1 "the bastions of taxation metamorphosed into columned palaces.":
Mercier, Louis-Sébastien. Le Tableau de Paris 1782-1788, 12 Vol. Translated
and abridged into English by Helen Simpson, Philadelphia: J. B. Lippincott
Co., 1933.

Bois de Vincennes

1 "Let us strangle the last king with the guts of the last priest.":Attributed
to Diderot by Jean-François de La Harpe in *Cours de Littérature Ancienne et
Moderne*, 1840.

Jardins du Ranelagh

1 "Three may keep a Secret, if two of them are dead.": Franklin, Benjamin.
Poor Richard's Almanac, 1735.

Bois de Boulogne

1 "Courage!... are to end?": Goodrich, Frank B. *Women of Beauty and
Heroism*, New York: Derby & Jackson, 1859.

Chapter 23: Bibliography

Readers wishing to pursue their own readings on the history of Paris and its parks and gardens will find the following general sources a good beginning. Susan Cahill's, *Hidden Gardens of Paris* (New York: St. Martin's Griffin Press, 2012), is an excellent first read in English. Anne Soprani's, *Jardins: Promenade historique dans les parcs et jardins de chaque arrondissement* (Paris: Éditions Paris-Méditerranée, 1998) was a constant companion for the research. My second-best source was Bernard Champigneulle's, *Promenades dans les Jardins de Paris, Ses Bois, et Ses Squares* (Paris: Club des Libraires de France, 1965).

While in Paris, Sabine Jeanin's (ed.), *Les Parcs et Jardins de Paris: 400 lieux de détente et de decouverte* (Paris: Rustica Edition, 2001) was a daily reference guide to the Paris park system. Dominique Jarrassé's, *Grammaire des Jardins Parisiens* (Paris: Parigramme Publishers, 2007) and Patrice De Moncan's, *Les Jardins du Baron Haussmann* (Paris: Les Éditions du Mécène, 2009) are both excellent readings on the current Paris park system.

My principal sources for the Revolution of 1789 were Thomas Carlyle's, *The French Revolution: A History*, (Boston: Little & Brown, 1838) and Simon Schama's, *Citizens*, (New York: Alfred A. Knopf, 1989).

Three texts that offer detailed information on the history of Paris as related to the parks and gardens were Jacques Hillairet's, *Connaissance du vieux Paris Rive Gauche/Rive Droit/Les Îles et Les Villages* (Editions de Minuit, Paris: Editions Payot & Rivages pour la présente édition (1956), 1993), his *Dictionnaire historique des rues de Paris* (Paris: Les Éditions de Minuit, 1997), and Alfred Fierro's, *Histoire et Dictionnaire de Paris* (Paris: Robert Laffont S. A. Publ., 1996).

Eye-witness accounts of great historical events in the history of Paris offer readers a unique and intimate understanding. Two of my favorites are Thomas Blaikie's, *Diary of a Scotch Gardener at the French Court at the End of the Eighteenth Century.* (ed. Francis Birrell, London: George Rutledge & Sons, Ltd., 1931) and Poumiès de la Siboutie's, *Recollections of a Parisian under Six Sovereigns, Two Revolutions, and a Republic* (Branche, A. and L. Dagoury, ed. translated by Lady Theodora Davidson, London: John Murray Publishers, 1911). Blaikie's memories of the first months of the Revolution of 1789 are full of high drama and poignancy, while Siboute's memoires offer a long-term rather cynical view of French politics over many decades covering the Empire and the Revolutions of 1830 and 1848.

If the reader wishes to cover Paris history in a single volume, Colin Jones's, *Paris: A Biography of a City* (London: Penguin Books, 2004) is a scholastic achievement of the first order.

Numbered source notes for each chapter accompany the bibliography.

Abbo, Cernuus. (N. Dass ed.) *Viking Attacks on Paris: The Bella Parisiacae Urbis of Abbo of Saint-Germain-des-Prés*, Louvain: Peeters Publishers, 2007.

Abbott, Jacob. *Early Aeronautics*, New York: Harpers/Folly Cove Press, 1869.

Abulhon, Maurice. *The French Republic 1879–1992*, Oxford: Blackwell, 1993.

Aldis, Janet. *The Queen of Letter-Writers*, London: Metheun and Co. and New York: G. P. Putnam's Sons, 1907.

Allwood, John. *The Great Exhibitions*, London: Cassell & Collier Macmillan Publishers, 1977.

Anderson, Lonzo. *Bag of smoke: The story of the first balloon*, New York: Knopf, 1942.

Andress, David. *The Terror: The Merciless War for Freedom in Revolutionary France*, New York: Farrar, Straus & Giroux, 2004.

Argenson, Marquis Rene-Louis De Voyer. *Journal and Memoirs of the Marquis D'Argenson. Volumes 1 and 2, Published from the autograph mss*. Musée du Louvre by E. J. B. Rathery, Introduction by E. A. Sainte-Bouve, Translated by Katherine Scott Wormely, Boston: Hardy Pratt and Company, 1902.

Ashley, Maurice P. *Louis XIV and The Greatness of France*, New York: The Free Press (Simon and Schuster), 1965.

Asprey, R. B. *The First Battle of the Marne*, London: Weidenfeld & Nicholson, 1962.

Auchincloss, Louis. *Richelieu*, New York: Viking Press, 1972.

Ayers, Andrew. *The Architecture of Paris*, Stuttgart: Edition Axel Menges, 2004.

Baker, Mark A. *Spies of Revolutionary Connecticut, From Benedict Arnold to Nathan Hale*, Seattle: The History Press (Amazon Digital Services), 2014.

Barber, Malcolm. *The New Knighthood: A History of the Order of the Temple.* Cambridge: Cambridge University Press, 1994.

Barber, Malcolm. *The Trial of the Templars*, Cambridge: Cambridge University Press, 1978.

Barbier, Patrick. *Opera in Paris, 1800–1850: A Lively History*, Portland: Amadeus Press, 1995.

Barthélemy, E. De. *Gazette de la Régence: Janvier 1715-Juin 1719*, Charleston: Nabu Press, 2014.

Bartlett, David W. *Paris with Pen and Pencil its People and Literature and Life and Business*, New York: Butler Brothers, Inc., 1858.

Baxter, John. *Paris at the End of the World: The City of Light during the Great War, 1914–1918.* New York: Harper Perennial, 2014.

Belloc, Hilaire. *Richelieu: A Study*, London: J. B. Lippincott, 1929.

Beraud, Henri. *Twelve Portraits of the French Revolution*, New York: Books for Library Press, Inc., 1928.

Bernhardt, Sarah. *Memoirs of My Life*, New York: Bloom, LOC No. 68-56475, 1908.

Bernier, Olivier. *Louis XIV: A Royal Life*, New York: Doubleday, 1987.

Berthaud, Sieur. *La Ville de Paris en vers burlesques*, Derniere Edition, Augmentée de la Foire Saint Germain. Paris: Chez Esstienne Leyson, au Palais, dans la Gallerie des Prifonniers, au Nom de Iefus, 1661.

Blaikie, Thomas. *Diary of a Scotch Gardener at the French Court at the End of the Eighteenth Century*, (ed. Francis Birrell), London: George Rutledge & Sons, Ltd., 1931.

Bolt, Marvin. *The Biographical Encyclopedia of Astronomers*, JoAnn Palmeri (Adapter), Thomas Hockey (Editor), Virginia Trimble (Editor), Thomas R. Williams (Editor), Katherine Bracher (Editor), Richard Jarrell (Editor), Jordan D. Marché (Editor), F. Jamil Ragep (Editor), Berlin: Springer, 2007.

Bonaparte, Napoleon. *Napoleon: In His Own Words*, From the French of Jules Bertaut, Translated by H. E. Law and C. L. Rhodes, Chicago: A. C. McClurg and Co. 1916.

Bonifacio, Antoine and Paul Maréchal. *La France, l'Europe et le monde, de 1715 à 1870*, Paris: Hachette, 1965.

Bouchoux, Corinne. *Rose Valland: résistance au musée*, Paris: La Crèche: Geste, 2006.

Bourdon, David and Bernard de Montgolfier. *Christo: The Pont Neuf Wrapped, Paris, 1975-85*, (Photographs by Wolfgang Volz. Abrams), New York: DuMont, 1990.

Bown, Matthew, and Matteo Lanfranconi. *Socialist Realisms: Great Soviet Painting 1920-1970*, New York: Skira Rizzoli Publishing, 2012.

Braham, Alan. *The Architecture of the French Enlightenment*, Berkley: University of California Press, 1989.

Brinnin, John Malcom. *The Third Rose: Gertrude Stein and Her World*, Addison-Wesley, Reading, Mass. 1987.

Brooks, Richard. *Atlas of World Military History*, London: HarperCollins, 2000.

Buckley, Veronica. *Madame de Maintenon: The Secret Wife of Louis XIV*, London: Bloomsbury Press, 2008.

Bull, Gerald V. and Charles H. Murphy. *Paris Kanonen: The Paris Guns (Wilhelmgeschutze) and Project HARP*, Herford: E. S. Mittler, 1988.

Burman, Edward. *The Templars: Knights of God*, Rochester: Destiny Books, 1990.

Butler, Alan and Stephen Dafoe. *The Warriors and the Bankers: A History of the Knights Templar from 1307 to the present*, Belleville: Templar Books, 1998.

Buvat, Jean. Journal *La Régence (14.3.1719)*, Notes et d'un Index Alphabetique par Emile Campardon Archiviste aux Archives de l'Empire. Vol. 2, Paris: Plon, Imprimeur-Éditeur, 1865.

Cain, George, and A. R. Richard. *Walks in Paris*, translated by Alfred Allinson, New York: Macmillan and Sons, 1909.

_____. *Nooks and Corners of Old Paris* (2nd ed.), London: The Richards Press Ltd., 1928.

____, George. *The Byways of Paris*, (translated by Louise Seymour Houghton), originally published by Duffield,1912, Whitefish (MT): Kessinger Publishing, LLC, 2010.

Carcopino, J. *Daily Life in Ancient Rome*, (copyright 1941), New Haven: Yale University Press, 2003.

Carlyle, Thomas. *The French Revolution: A*. 1837, The Project Gutenberg EBook of The French Revolution: A History, 1837.

Caro, Ina. *Paris to the Past: Traveling through French History by Train*, New York: W.W. Norton & Company, 2012.

Castelot, Andre. Paris: *The Turbulent City 1783-1787*, (translated by Denise Folliot and Barrie Rockliff with Vallentine Michell), New York: Harper and Row, 1962.with Vallentine Michell), New York: Harper and Row, 1962.

Catel, Emmanuelle Polack, and Claire Bouilhac. *The Monuments Men and The Train, Rose Valland*. [Marcinelle (Belgique)]: Dupuis, 2009.

Chabin, Marie-Anne. *L'astronome français Joseph-Nicolas Delisle à la cour de Russie dans la première moitié du XVIIIe siècle, in L'influence française en Russie au XVIIIe siècle*, ed. Jean-Pierre Poussou, Anne Mézin, and Yves Perret-Gentil, Institut d'Études Slaves, Paris: Presses de l'Université de Paris-Sorbonne, 2004.

Chastenet, Jacques. *Cent Ans de la République*, Paris: Librairie Jules Tallandier, 1970.

Chernow, Burt. *Christo and Jeanne-Claude: A Biography*, New York: St. Martin's Press, 2002.

Chisholm, Hugh (Ed.). *Marquise de Sévigné, Marie de Rabutin-Chantal*, Encyclopædia Britannica 24 (11th ed.). Cambridge: Cambridge University Press, 1911.

_____, Hugh, ed. *Louis Petit de Bachaumont, Encyclopædia Britannica* (11th ed.). Cambridge: Cambridge University Press, 1911.

Christophe, Robert. *Les Sanson, bourreaux de père en fils, pendant deux siècles*, Paris: Arthème Fayard, 1960.

Cobban, Alfred. *A History of Modern France*, London: Penguin Books, 1965.

Cody, William F. *An Autobiography of Buffalo Bill Cody*, Tom Thomas (ed.), Seattle: CreateSpace Independent Publishing Platform, 2010.

Cole, Hubert. First Gentleman of the Bedchamber: The Life of Louis-François-Armand, Maréchal Duc de Richelieu, New York: Viking Press, 1965.

Colette, Sidonie Garbielle. *Paris de ma fenétre*. Geneva: Editions du Milieu du Monde, 1944.

Collins, Larry and Dominique Lapierre. *Is Paris Burning?* New York: Simon and Schuster, Inc. 1965.

Combeau, Yvan. *Histoire de Paris*, Paris: Presses universitaires de France (PUF), 7th edition, 2011.

Commines, Philippe de. *Memoirs of the French Court: Phillipe de Commines, Marguerite de Valois, Duc de Sully, Cardinal de Richelieu, Cardinal de Retz, Madame de Montespan, Duc de Saint-Simon, Madame Campan, Madame Roland, Prince de Talleyrand, Madame de Remusat and Madame Junot*, With special introduction by George Saintsbury, New York: Colonial Press, Revised Edition P. F. Collier and Son, 1901.

Coulson, Thomas. *Mata Hari: Courtesan and Spy*, London: Hutchinson, 1930.

Cowart, Georgia J. *The Triumph of Pleasure: Louis XIV and the Politics of Spectacle*, Chicago: University of Chicago Press, 2008.

Cronin, Vincent. *Four Women in Pursuit of an Ideal*, London: Collins, 1965.

_____. *Louis XIV*, London: Harper Collins, 1996.

Crouch, David. *Tournament*. Sydney: Bloomsbury Academic, 2007.

Cuisin, J.-P.-R. *Les duels, suicides et amours du bois de Boulogne: Première et Seconde partie*, Paris: Ligaran Publishers, 2016.

Darnall, Diane Thomas. *The challengers: a century of ballooning*, Brisbane: Hunter Pub. Co., 1989.

Darwin, Charles. *On the Origin of Species. Or the Preservation of Favored Races in the Struggle for Life*, From the First Edition, London: John Murray, 1859.

Davis, Tom. *Lighter Than Air*, Baltimore: The Johns Hopkins University Press, 2009.

Demurger, Alain. *The Last Templar - The Tragedy of Jacques de Molay, Last Grand Master of the Temple*, (Translated into English by Antonia Nevill), London: Profile Books LTD, (First publication in France in 2002 as Jacques de Molay: le crépuscule des templiers by Éditions Payot & Rivages), 2004.

Devêche, André. *The Tuileries Palace and Gardens*, (translated by Jonathan Eden) Paris: Éditions de la Tourelle-Maloine, 1981.

Dickinson, Henry Winram. *Robert Fulton, Engineer and Artist: His Life and Works*, Seattle: Ulan Press, 2012.

Doyle, William. *The Oxford History of the French Revolution*, Oxford: Oxford University Press; 2nd editions, 2003.

Druon, Maurice. *The History of Paris from Caesar to Saint Louis*, (translated by Humphrey Hare) London: Rupert-Davis, 1969.

Duhem, Jules. (Fernand Sorlot ed.) *Histoire des idéas aéronautiques avant Montgolfier*, Paris: Nouvelles Editions Latines, 1943.

Durant, Will and Ariel Durant. *The Age of Napoleon: A History of European Civilization from 1789 to 1815*, New York: MJF Books, 1975.

_____, Will and Ariel Durant. *The Story of Civilization: Volume 8, The Age of Louis XIV,* New York: Simon and Schuster, 1975.

Dussane, Béatrix. *La Comédie-Française*, French Edition, public domain reprint from 1923. Charleston: Nabu Press, 2010.

Duval, Amaury. *L'Evéque Gozlin ou le siege de Paris par les Normands, chronique du IX siècle, Paris, 1832.*

Edwards, Stewart. *The Paris Commune 1871*, London: Eyre & Spottiswoode, 1971.

Erlanger, Philippe, *Louis XIV*, Phoenix: Phoenix Press, 2003.

Fierro, Alfred. *Histoire et Dictionnaire de Paris*. Paris: Robert Laffont S. A. Publ., 1996.

Findling, John E., and Kimberly D. Pelle. *Encyclopedia of World's Fairs and Expositions*, Jefferson: McFarland Publishing, Reprint edition, 2015.

Fitzgerald, Robert. *The Iliad*, New York: Farrar, Straus and Giroux, 2004.

Flamel, Nicolas. *Theory and Practice of the Philosopher's Stone*, (reprint of 1624 version printed in London), Eastford: Martino Fine Books, 2009.

Flanner (Genêt), Janet. *Paris Journal 1944-1965*, (ed.) William Shawn, New York: Atheneum Publ., 1965.

Fleming, G. H. *James Abbott McNeill Whistler: A Life*, Adlestrop: Windrush, 1991.

_____. *The Young Whistler, 1834–66*, London: Allen and Unwin., 1978.

Fournel, Victor. *Curiosités théâtrales anciennes et modernes, françaises et étrangères*, Nouvelle Édition, Paris: Garnier Frères Librairies-Éditeurs, 1878.

Frale, Barbara. *The Chinon chart. Papal absolution to the last Templar, Master Jacques de Molay*, Journal of Medieval History, 30:2, 2004.

_____. *The Templars - The secret history revealed*, Dunboyne: Maverick House Publishers, 2009.

Fraser, Antonia. *Love and Louis XIV: The Women in the Life of the Sun King.* London: Weidenfeld & Nicolson, 2006.

Galignani, A.A and W. Galignani . *The History of Paris V2: From the Earliest Period to The Present Day (1825),* London: Kessinger Publishing, LLC, 2009.

Gates, D. *The Napoleonic Wars, 1803–1815*, New York: Pimlico (RAND). 2003.

Georgano, G. N. *Cars: Early and Vintage, 1886-1930*, London: Grange-Universal, (reprints AB Nordbok 1985 edition), 1990.

Geppert, Alexander C. T. *Fleeting Cities. Imperial Expositions in Fin-de-Siècle Europe*, Basingstoke/New York: Palgrave Macmillan, 2010.

Gibbon, Edward and David P. Womersley. *The History of the Decline and Fall of the Roman Empire*, London: Penguin Classics, Abridged edition, 2001.

Gibbons, Helen Davenport. *Paris Vistas*, With sixteen illustrations by Lester George Hornby, New York: The Century Co., 1919.

Gillispie, Charles. *The Montgolfier Brothers, and the Invention of Aviation*, Princeton: Princeton University Press, 1983.

Glass, Charles. *Americans in Paris: Life and Death under Nazi Occupation*, London: The Penguin Press, 2010.

Glyn, Anthony. *Great Rivers of the World: The Seine*, New York: G.P. Putnam's Sons, 1967.

Goubert, Pierre. *Louis XIV and Twenty Million Frenchmen*, Translated by Anne Carter, New York: Vintage Books, 1972.

Goyau, Pierre-Louis-Théophile-Georges. *Jules Mazarin*, Catholic Encyclopedia, Volume 10, 1913.

Grant, Michael. *Gladiators*, New York: Barnes & Noble, Inc. (by arrangement with Michael Grant Publications Ltd. 1967), 1995.

Gray, Francine Du plessix. *At Home with the Marquis De Sade: A Life*, New York: Simon & Schuster, 1998.

Greenhalgh, Paul. *Fair World: A History of World's Fairs and Expositions from London to Shanghai 1851-2010*, Auckland: Papadakis Dist A C, 2011.

Gregory, Bishop of Tours. *History of the Franks*, Translated by Ernest Brehaut, New York: Octagon Books, Farrar, Straus, and Giroux, 1973.

Grene, David. *The Histories of Herodotus*, Chicago: University of Chicago Press, 1985.

Grishin, A. A. *The Knights Templar Absolution: The Chinon Parchment and the History of the Poor Knights of Christ*, Las Vegas: On Demand Publishing LLC, CreateSpace, 2013.

Haag, Michael. *The Templars: History and Myth*, London: Profile Books Ltd., 2008.

____, Michael. *The Tragedy of the Templars*, London: Profile Books Ltd., 2012.

Hackett, Francis. *Francis the First*, Garden City: Doubleday, Doran, & Co., Inc., 1937.

Hamerton, Philip Gilbert. *Paris: Old and Present Times With special reference to changes in its architecture and topography*, Boston: Little, Brown and Co., 1885, 1900.

Harrison, James A. *Letters of Madame de Sévigné*, Boston: Ginn & Co, 1899.

Hassall, Arthur. *Mazarin*, London: Macmillan and Company, 1903.

Hauck, Dennis William. *Socerer's Stone: A Beginner's Guide to Alchemy*, Seattle: CreateSpace Independent Publishing Platform; Second edition, 2013.

Hautecoeur, Louis. *L'Histoire des Chateaux du Louvre et des Tuileries*, Paris: G. Van Oest, 1927.

Head, Sir Francis. *A Faggot of French Sticks; or, Paris in 1851*, Two volumes complete in one., New York: George E. Putnam, 1851.

Hemingway, Ernest. *The Moveable Feast*, New York: Charles Scribner and Sons, 1964.

Héron de Villefosse, René. *Histoire de Paris*, Paris: Bernard Grasset, 1959.

Herwig, H. *The Marne, 1914: The Opening of World War I and the Battle that Changed the World*, New York: Random House, 2009.

Hibbert, Christopher. *The Days of the French Revolution*, New York: William Morrow and Co., 1980.

Hillairet, Jacques. *Connaissance du vieux Paris Rive Gauche/Rive Droit/Les Îles et Les Villages*, Editions de Minuit, Paris: Editions Payot & Rivages pour la présente édition (1956),1993.

_____. *Connaissance du vieux Paris: Rive Gauche/Rive Droit/Les Îles et Les Villages*, Editions de Minuit, Paris, 1993.

_____.. *Dictionnaire historique des rues de Paris*, Paris: Les Éditions de Minuit, 1997.

Hobhouse, Janet. *Everybody Who Was Anybody: A Biography of Gertrude Stein*, New York: G. P. Putnam's Sons, 1975.

Hoog, Michael. *The Nympheas of Claude Monet at the Musee De l'Orangerie*, Paris: Reunion Des Musées Nationaux, 1990.

Horne, Alistair. *To Lose a Battle: France 1940*, London: Penguin Books, 1979.

Howe, Russell Warren. *Mata Hari: The True Story*, New York: Dodd, Mead, & Co., 1986.

Hugo, Victor, and Lee Fahnestock (Translator, Introduction), *Les Misérables*, New York: Signet, 1862, Signet edition, 2013.

_____. *Les Misérables*, translated by Isabel F. Hapgood, The Project Gutenberg EBook of Les Misérables, EBook #135. New York: Thomas Y. Crowell & Co., 1887.

Jackson, Anna. Expo: *International Expositions 1851-2010*, London: V & A Publishing, 2008.

Jackson, Donald Dale. *The Aeronauts*, New York: Time-Life Books, 1980.

Jackson, Julian. *The Fall of France: The Nazi Invasion of 1940*, Oxford: Oxford University Press, 2004.

Jacob, Paul Lacroix. *Curiosités de l'histoire du vieux Paris (1858),* Paris: Adolphe Delahays Libraire-Éditeur, 1858.

Jacques de Molay, *The Catholic Encyclopedia*, New York: Robert Appleton Company, Retrieved 8 January, 2010.

Jacquin, Emmanuel. *Les Tuileries, Du Louvre à la Concorde*, Paris: Editions du Patrimoine, Centres des Monuments Nationaux, 1997.

James, E. *The Franks*, Oxford: Oxford University Press, 1988.

_____. *The Origins of France*, Palgrave Macmillan, 1989.

Jarrassé, Dominique. *Grammaire des Jardins Parisiens*, Paris: Parigramme Publishers, 2007.

Jeanin, Sabine (ed.). *Les Parcs et Jardins de Paris: 400 lieux de détente et de decouverte*, Paris: Rustica Edition, 2001.

Jones, Colin. *Paris: A Biography of a City*, London: Penguin Books, 2004.

Jonnes Jill. *Eiffel's Tower: The Thrilling Story Behind Paris's Beloved Monument and the Extraordinary World's Fair That Introduced It*, London: Penguin, 2010.

Jordan, David E. *The King's Trial: The French Revolution Vs. Louis XVI*, Berkeley: University of California Press; First Edition, Twenty-fifth Anniversary Edition, 2004.

Kargon, Robert H., Karen Fiss, Morris Low, and Arthur P. Molella. *World's Fairs on the Eve of War: Science, Technology, and Modernity, 1937-1942*, Pittsburgh: University of Pittsburgh Press, 2015.

Khan, Yasmin Sabina. *Enlightening the world: the creation of the Statue of Liberty*, Ithaca: Cornell University Press, 2010.

Klossowski. *The 120 Days of Sodom and Other Writings*, New York: Grove Press, 1994.

Knecht, R.J. *Renaissance Warrior and Patron: The Reign of Francis I*, Cambridge: Cambridge University Press, 1994.

Knight, Randall D. *Physics for Scientists and Engineers*, (2nd ed.) Harlow Essex: Addison-Wesley, 2007.

Kotar, S. L., and J. E. Gessler. *Ballooning: A History, 1782-1900*, Jefferson: McFarland Publishing, 2010.

Kurtz, Harold. *The Trial of Marshal Ney: His Last Years and Death*, New York: Alfred A. Knopf, 1957.

La Fontaine, Jean de. *Fables of La Fontaine, A New Edition with Notes*, Translated from the French by Elizur Wright by J. W. M. Gibbs. 1882. Project Gutenberg's The Fables of La Fontaine, by Jean de la Fontaine, EBook #7241.

La Revue Hebdomadaire. Douzième Année, Vol. 5, Paris: Plon-Nourrit et C., Imprimeurs-Éditeurs, April, 1903.

Lambert, Guy, Dominique Massounie, and Jean-Christophe Ballot. *The Palais-Royal*, Paris: editions du Patrimoine, Centre des monuments nationaux, 2008.

Latham, Edward. *Famous Sayings and their Authors: A Collection of Historical Sayings in English, French, German, Greek, Italian, And Latin*, London: Swan Sonnenschein and Co. Lim. 1906.

Latour, Thérèse Louis. *Princesses, Ladies, and Republicans of the Terror*, New York: Alfred A. Knopf, 1930.

Laughlin, Clara E. *So You're Going to Paris*, 5th edition, New York: The Riverside Press, 1930.

Le Gallienne, Charles Hanson. *From a Paris Garret*, New York: Ives Washburn Publisher, 1936.

_____. *From a Paris Scrapbook*, New York: Ives Washburn Publisher, 1938.

Le Hallé, Guy. *Histoire des fortifications de Paris et leur extension en Île-de-France*, Paris: Éditions Horvath, 1995.

Le Petit, Claude. *Paris ridicule et burlesque au dix-septième siècle*, (Nouvelle édition revue et corrigée par P. L. Jacob bibliophile), Paris: Adolphe Delahays, libraire-éditeur, 1859.

Leggiere, Michael V. *The Fall of Napoleon: The Allied Invasion of France, 1813-1814*. (Cambridge: Cambridge University Press, 2007.

Lelong, Guy. Daniel Buren, *Paris*: Group Flammarion, 2002.

Lenotre, George. *La vie à Paris pendant la Revolution: 1789-1793*, Paris: Calmann-Levy, 1961.

Levi, Anthony. *Cardinal Richelieu and the Making of France*, New York: Carroll and Graf, 2000.

Lissagaray, Prosper-Olivier. *Histore de la Commune de 1871*, Paris: La Decouverte/Poche, 2000.

Lister, Martin. *A Journey to Paris in the Year 1698*, first published in 1698, Urbana: Reprinted University of Illinois Press, 1967.

Lobet, J. *Le Nouveau Bois de Boulogne: et Ses Alentours, Histoire, Description et Souvenirs*, Ouvrage Illustré de 26 Vignettes par Thérond, Paris: Librairie de L. Hachette et Co., 1856.

Longstreet, Stephen. *We All Went to Paris: Americans in the City of Light 1776-1971*, Barnes & Noble; 1st edition, 2004.

Loomis, Stanley. *Paris in the Terror: June 1793-July 1794*, Philadelphia: J. B. Lippincott Company, 1965.

Lucas, E. V. *A Wanderer in Paris*, London: 15th Edition, Methuen & Co., Ltd., 1909.

Lucas, John. *The Big Umbrella*, London: Drake Publishers Inc., 1973.

Mabillon, Dom. Joannes. *The Complete Works of Saint Bernard, Abbot of Clairvaux*, translated by Dr. Samuel John Eales, London: John Hodges, 1904.

MacLean, Simon. *Kingship and Politics in the Late Ninth Century: Charles the Fat and the end of the Carolingian Empire*, Cambridge University Press, 2003.

Malcolm, Janet. *Two Lives: Gertrude and Alice*, London: Yale University Press, 2007.

Mallgrave, Harry Francis. *Architectural Theory: An Anthology from Vitruvius to 1870*, London: Blackwell Publishing, 2005.

Mandell, Richard D. *Paris 1900: The Great World's Fair*, Toronto: University of Toronto Press, 1967.

Marcellinus, Ammianus. *Res Gestae, Libri XV-XXV (books 15–25)*, See J.C. Rolfe, Ammianus Marcellinus, 3 Volumes, Cambridge: Harvard University Press, 1935/1985.

Marcellinus, Ammianus. *The Roman History of Ammianus Marcellinus During the Reigns of the Emperors Constantius, Julian, Jovianus, Valentinian, and Valens*, Translated by C. D. Yonge. Salt Lake City: Gutenberg etext# 28587, 2009.

Martin, Henry. *Histoire de la Bibliothèque de l'arsenal*, Paris: E. Plon, Nourrit et Cie, 1900.

Mattie Erik. *World's Fairs*, Princeton: Princeton Architectural Press, 1998.

Maurice, Arthur Bartlett. *The Paris of the Novelists*, New York: Doubleday, Page, and Co., 1919.

Mayr, Ernst. *The Growth of Biological Thought*, Cambridge: Harvard University Press,1981.

McCullough, David. *Americans in Paris, The Greater Journey*, New York: Simon and Schuster, 2011.

Mellor, C. Michael. *Louis Braille: A Touch of Genius*, Boston: National Braille Press, 2006.

Melville, Herman. *Moby Dick or The Whale*, New York: Harper and Brothers, 1851.

Mercier, Louis-Sébastien. *Le Tableau de Paris 1782-1788*, 12 Vol. Translated and abridged into English by Helen Simpson, Philadelphia: J. B. Lippincott Co., 1933.

Michelet, Jules. *Histoire de France*, Vols 1-10, Seattle: Amazon Digital Services, 2015.

Miller, Henry W. *The Paris Gun: The Bombardment of Paris by the German Long-Range Guns and the Great German Offensive of 1918*, New York: Jonathan Cape, Harrison Smith, 1930.

Misencik, Paul R. *The Original American Spies: Seven Covert Agents of The Revolutionary War*, Charlotte: North Carolina-McFarland Publishing, 2013.

Mitchell, Allan. *Nazi Paris: The History of an Occupation 1940-1944*, New York: Berghahn Books, 2008.

Mitford, Nancy. *The Sun King*, New York: NYRB Classics, 2012.

Mossiker, Francis. *Madame de Sévigne: A Life and Letters*, New York, Columbia University Press, 1985.

_____. *The Affair of the Poisons: Louis XIV, Madame de Montespan, and One of History's Great Unsolved Mysteries*, New York: Alfred A. Knopf, 1969.

Murdoch, Adrian. *The Last Pagan: Julian the Apostate and the Death of the Ancient World*, Gloucestershire: Stroud, 2005.

Nagy, John A. *Invisible Ink – Spy craft of the American Revolution*, Seattle: Westholme Publishing (Amazon Digital Services), 2011.

Neander, August. *The Emperor Julian and His Generation, An Historical Picture*, (translated by G.V. Cox), London: John W. Parker, 1850.

Nicholson, Helen. *The Knights Templar: A New History*, Stroud: Sutton, 2001.

O'Connell, D.P. *Richelieu*, New York: The World Publishing Company, 1968.

Ogrizek, Doré. (ed.) *The Paris We Love*, Introduction by Jean Cocteau, Chapter: The Plaine Monceau, By Jean-Louis Vaudoyer, illustrated by Philippe Jullian, New York: McGraw-Hill Co., Inc., 1950.

Ostrovsky, Erika. *Eye of Dawn: The Rise and Fall of Mata Hari*, New York: Macmillan, 1978.

Parkinson, Helen. 2020. *Vosges*. France 161:60–61.

Pascal, Blaise, *Pensées and Other Writings*, Translated by Honor Levi. (ed.) Anthony Levi. Oxford: Oxford Paperbacks, 2008.

_____. *Pensées*, Translated by A. J. Krailsheimer, London: Penguin Classics, 1995.

Pearl, Cora. *Grandes Horizontales: The lives and legends of Marie Duplessis, La Paiva, and La Presidente*, New York: Virginia Rounding, Bloomsbury Publishers, 2003.

Pellissier, Georges. *The Literary Movement in France During the Nineteenth Century*, Authorized English Version by Ann Garrison Brinton, New York and London: G. P. Putnams Sons, 1897.

Perkins, James Breck. *France Under Mazarin* (2 volumes), New York: Putnam, 1886

Perris, George Herbert. *The Battle of the Marne*, London: Methuen and Co. Ltd., 1920.

Petitfils, Jean-Christian. *Crime et sorcellerie au temps du roi soleil*, Paris: Perrin, 2010.

Philip, Cynthia. *Robert Fulton: A Biography*, Bloomington: iUniverse, 2003.

Pitou, Spire. *The Paris Opéra: an encyclopedia of operas, ballets, composers, and performers* (3 volumes), vol. 1. Westport: Greenwood Press, 1983.

Polack, d'Emmanuelle et Philippe Dagen, *Les carnets de Rose Valland: Le pillage des collections privées d'oeuvres d'art en France durant la Seconde Guerre Mondiale*, Paris: Fage Editions, 2011.

Prevot, Philippe. *Histoire des jardins*, Paris: Editions Sud-Ouest, 2006.

Read, Piers. *The Templars*, New York: Da Capo Press, 2001.

Renaud Gagneux et Denis Prouvost, *Sur les traces des enceintes de Paris*, Parigramme, 2004.

Richardson, Joanna. *Paris under Siege*, London: Folio Society London, 1982.

Riding, Alan. *And the Show Went On: Cultural Life in Nazi-occupied Paris*, New York: Alfred A. Knopf, 2011.

Robb, Graham. *Parisians: An Adventure History of Paris*, London: Picador, 2010.

Roberts, Kate Louise. *Hoyt's New Cyclopedia of Practical Quotations*, New York And London: Funk & Wagnalls Company, 1922.

Roob, Alexander. *Alchemy & Mysticism*. Los Angeles: Taschen, 2014.

Rosbottom, Ronald C. *When Paris Went Dark: The City of Light under German Occupation 1940–1944*, New York: Little, Brown and Company, 2014.

Rosbottom, Ronald C. *When Paris Went Dark: The City of Light under German Occupation 1940–1944*, New York: Little, Brown and Company, 2014.

Ross, Kristin. *May '68 and Its Afterlives*, Chicago: University of Chicago Press, first edition, 2004.

Rougerie, Jacques. *Paris libre 1871*, Paris: Editions du Seuil, 2004.

Rounding, Virginia. *Grandes Horizontales: The lives and legends of Marie Duplessis, Cora Pearl, La Paiva and La Presidente*, New York: Bloomsbury Publishers, 2003.

Rowling, J. K. *Harry Potter and the Philosopher's Stone*. Vancouver: Raincoast, 1998.

Russell, John. *Paris*, Harry N. Abrams, Inc., Publishers, New York, 1983.

Sala, George Augustus. *Paris Herself Again, 1878-79 in London Daily Telegraph*, London: Golden Galley Press Limited, 1948.

Schaeffer, Neil. *The Marquis de Sade: A Life*, New York: Knopf, 1999.

Schama, Simon. *Citizens: A Chronicle of the French Revolution*, New York: Vintage Books, 1990.

Scott, Michael. *The Alchemyst: The Secrets of the Immortal Nicholas Flamel*. Bel Air: Ember Publ., 2008.

Sébastien-Roch, Nicolas. *Œuvres completes de Chamfort, recueillies et publiées, avec une notice historique sur la vie et les écrits de l'auteur, par p. r. auguis.*, tome premier. paris. chez chaumerot jeune, libraire, palais-royal, galeries de bois, no 189. 1824.

Seward, Desmond. *François I: Prince of the Renaissance*, New York: MacMillan Publishing Co., 1973.

Shakespeare, William. *The Chronicle History of Henry the Fifth*. London: Thomas Creede, Thos. Millington and John Busby, 1600.

Shipman, Pat. *Femme Fatale: Love, Lies, and the Unknown Life of Mata Hari*, London: Weidenfeld & Nicolson, 2007.

Shirer, William L. *The Collapse of the Third Republic*, New York: Simon and Schuster, 1969.

Shirer, William L. *The Rise and Fall of the Third Reich: A History of Nazi Germany*, Reissue Edition, New York: Simon and Schuster, 2011.

Siboutie, de la, Poumiès. *Recollections of a Parisian under Six Sovereigns, Two Revolutions, and a Republic*, Branche, A. and L. Dagoury. (ed.), translated by Lady Theodora Davidson, London: John Murray Publishers, 1911.

Simons, Fraser. *The Early History of Ballooning—The Age of the Aeronaut*, Paris: Macha Press, 2014.

Singer, Daniel. *Prelude to Revolution: France in May 1968*, Chicago: Haymarket Books, second edition, 2013.

Skinner, Cornelia Otis. *Elegant Wits and Grand Horizontals*, Boston: The Riverside Cambridge Press, Houghton Mifflin Co., 1962.

_____. *Madame Sarah*, Boston: Houghton Mifflin Co., 1967.

Skuy, David. *Assassination, power, and miracle: France and the Royalist reaction of 1820*, Oxford: Queen's University Press, 2003.

Soden, Garrett. *Defying Gravity: Land Divers, Roller Coasters, Gravity Bums, and the Human Obsession with Falling*, New York: W. W. Norton & Company, 2005.

Somerset, Anne. *The Affairs of the Poisons: Murder, Infanticide, and Satanism at the Court of Louis XIV*, New York: St Martin's Press, 2003.

Soprani, Anne 1998, *Jardins: Promenade historique dans les parcs et jardins de chaque arrondissement*, Paris: Éditions Paris-Méditerranée, 1998.

_____. *Christo and Jeanne-Claude: 40 Years - 12 Exhibitions*, exh. cat. Annely Juda Fine Art, London, Great Britain, 2011.

_____, Anne. *Jardins: Promenade historique dans les parcs et jardins de chaque arrondissement*, Paris: Éditions Paris-Méditerranée, 1998.

Speer, Albert. *Inside the Third Reich*, (reissue edition), New York: Simon and Schuster, 1997.

Stein, Gertrude. *Geography and Plays*, Boston: The Four Seas Co. Publ. 1922.

_____. *Three Lives*, New York: Grafton Press, 1909.

Sumner, I. *The First Battle of the Marne 1914: The French 'miracle' Halts the Germans, Campaign*. Oxford: Osprey, 2010.

Swartwout Annie Fern. *Missie: The Life and Times of Annie Oakley*, Darke County, OH: Coachwhip Publications, 2013.

Thackery, William Makepeace. *The Paris Sketch Book of Mr. M. A. Titmarsh*, London: Dodo Press, 1840.

Thieme, Hugo P. *Woman in All Ages and in All Countries: Women of Modern France*, Philadelphia: The Rittenhouse Press, 1908.

Thomas, Elisabeth Finley. *The Paris We Remember*, Introduction by Elliot Paul, New York: D. Appleton-Century Co., Inc., 1942.

Thompson, Ian. *The Sun King's Garden: Louis XIV, André Le Nôtre And the Creation of the Gardens of Versailles*, London: Bloomsbury Publishing, 2006.

Tissandier, Gaston and Christopher d'James. *The Eiffel Tower*, Seattle: CreateSpace Independent Publishing Platform, 2012.

Treasure, Geoffrey. *Mazarin: The Crisis of Absolutism in France*, London: Routledge Publishers, 1995.

Treasure, Geoffrey. *Richelieu and Mazarin*, London: Routledge, 1998.

Tulloch, Principal. *Pascal, Provincial Letters, Letter XVI* (4 December 1656) Edinburgh and London: William Blackwood And Sons, 1878.—reprint, 1882.

Vandam, Albert D. *An Englishman in Paris*, New York: D. Appleton and Co., 1892.

Vidler, Anthony. Claude-Nicolas Ledoux, *Architecture and Social Reform at the End of the Ancien Régime*, Cambridge: The MIT Press, 1990.

Wales, Henry G. *Death Comes to Mata Hari*, San Francisco: International News Sevice, 1917.

Walsh, William. *A Handy Book of Curious Information*, London: Lippincott, 1913.

Wellman, Kathleen. *Queens and Mistresses of Renaissance France*, Hartford: Yale University Press, 2013.

Whittaker, G. B.: *The History of Paris from the Earliest Period to the Present Day*, Vol. II. p. 474 – 477 London: Printed for Geo. B. Whittaker and A. and W. Galignani (Paris), 1825.

Williams, H. Noel. *The Fascinating Duc De Richelieu, Louis Francois Armand Du Plessis 1696-1788*, London: Methuen and Co., Ltd., 1910.

Willms, Johannes. *Paris: Capitol of Europe from the Revolution to the Belle Epoque*. translated by Eveline L. Kanes. (Originally published under title, Paris: Hauptstadt Europas 1789-1914, C.H. Beck, Munich, 1988), New York: Holmes and Meier Publ. Inc., 1997.

Wise, David Burgess. *De Dion: The Aristocrat and the Toymaker*, in Ward, Ian, executive editor. *The World of Automobiles*, London: Orbis Publishing, 1974.

Wiser, William. *The Crazy Years: Paris in the Twenties*, London: Thames and Hudson Inc., 1983.

Wood, Ian. *The Merovingian Kingdoms 450–751*, London: Longman Group UK Limited, 1994.

Wright, Elizur. *The Battle of the Rats and the Weasels*, New Edition with notes, London: J. W. M. Gibbs 1882.

Wykeham, Peter. Santos Dumont: A Study in Obsession, New York:Harcourt,Brace & World,

Young, Alan. *Tudor and Jacobean Tournaments*, Chelsea: Sheridan House, 1998.

Young, Arthur. *Travels in France during the Years 1787, 1788, 1789,1792*, Current edition (ed.): Jeffry Kaplow, Gloucester: Peter Smith Publishing, 1976.

_____. *Travels in France during the Years 1787, 1788, 1789*, Edited by Jeffry Kaplow, 1792, Current edition: Gloucester: Peter Smith, 1976.

Ziegler, Gilette. *At the Court of Versailles: Eye-Witness Reports from the Reign of Louis XIV*, New York: E.P. Dutton & Co., Inc. 1966.

Index

James Bowers

About the Author

James Bowers is a retired oceanographer. After earning a Ph.D. from the University of Wisconsin James was a research scientist at the University of Michigan and the Savannah River National Laboratory. James and his wife share their time between Aiken, South Carolina and a village in Michigan.

Printed in Great Britain
by Amazon